vegetarian express

vegetarian
express

Rose Elliot

CASSELL&CO

First published in the United Kingdom in 2000
by Cassell & Co

Distributed in the United States of America
by Sterling Publishing Co., Inc.
387 Park Avenue South, New York,
NY 10016-8810

A CIP catalogue record for this book is available
from the British Library

3-8-02
$ 24.95

Designed by Lucy Holmes
Typesetting by Tiger Typeset

Printed and bound in Italy by Printer Trento S.r.l.

Cassell & Co
Wellington House
125 Strand
London WC2R 0BB

Contents

Introduction

Vegetarian Express is a book of fast recipes based on healthy, vitalizing ingredients. When you are busy and tired it is all too easy to grab a meal which, although quick, is full of fat, calories, and perhaps some rather dubious additives. It's filling and comforting at the time, but does nothing for health and energy levels. The recipes here are all simple and quick to make, and are based on fresh, natural ingredients, which are rich in vitamins and minerals. I have written them with an eye to fat and calorie content and supplied this information with each recipe so that you can keep track of it if you wish.

People have often asked me, on hearing that I'm vegetarian, "Doesn't it take much longer to make a meal?" I have to say that, honestly, it does not. Methods of preparation are different, and occasionally there are more ingredients to assemble, and it may take a little time to get used to this, but over all I am certain that vegetarian cooking can be just as fast as cooking with meat. And there are a number of advantages, one of these being that many staple foods keep very well, so you can do one big shop for these and then just top up with fresh items as necessary.

Another advantage of vegetarian food is that the raw ingredients—complex carbohydrates, such as pasta, rice, beans, lentils, fresh fruit and vegetables, nuts and seeds—are the very foods that nutritionists keep urging us all to eat for our good health. Perhaps that's why vegetarians have been found to be 30 per cent less likely to suffer from heart disease and some forms of cancer.

Of course, there are numerous other very sound reasons for being vegetarian. I believe that becoming vegetarian is a very personal decision, which is why it is not my style to try and convert anyone, but I do hope that people make that decision thoughtfully and don't go on eating meat just from habit. I'm vegetarian myself first and foremost because I do not want animals, birds, and fishes to be killed in order for me to eat, especially if they have been intensively reared in cruel conditions and brutally slaughtered.

As we move further into the 21st century there will be more and more pressure on world resources, such as land for growing crops and supplies of water. A vegetarian lifestyle, with its much lighter use of these resources, will become more and more appealing. If everyone became vegetarian we could feed the whole world several times over. Bearing in mind what I have already said about the reduction in disease, we would all be much healthier, too, with huge savings on health care. Becoming vegetarian is an independent, personal decision, but one that can have an important impact on the environment.

So, if you have just taken that decision, or are about to, and want the recipes to make it possible in your active life, welcome aboard the Vegetarian Express.

Fast food, healthy food

Fast, healthy cooking—indeed, any healthy cooking—begins with the right choice of ingredients: fresh, wholesome food for speedy, nutritious meals. The trick is to choose ingredients that, as well as being quick to prepare and cook, are also packed with vitamins and minerals. Along with these major nutrients, they also contain trace elements, antioxidants, fiber, and a whole variety of natural substances for radiant health. These ingredients are:

• Cereals and cereal products: oats, pasta, noodles, polenta, couscous, rice, and bread, especially whole wheat but including other types for variety; wheatgerm bread contains added B vitamins, for when you need de-stressing.

• Pulses—beans, garbanzos (chickpeas), and lentils—a nutritionist's dream food, are packed with goodness and low in fat. For high-speed cooking you will be using canned beans, preferably without added sugar or, if you are very well organized, you will have soaked, cooked, and frozen the beans in advance. A 1-pound package of dried beans or garbanzos, when soaked and cooked, makes five portions, each equivalent to a 14-ounce can. Dried split red/orange lentils can be used straight from the package as they cook in 20 minutes.

• Soy milk and bean curd are made from soy beans and thus belong to the pulse group, but are so useful that they deserve a category of their own.

• Vegetables of all kinds, including, for tip-top health, a serving of dark green leafy ones every day. Broccoli and the rest of the cabbage family are particularly good. A meal of "veg-and-two-veg" is one of the healthiest: potatoes make great main courses; frozen peas are not to be despised as an accompanying vegetable or to make into soup; canned tomatoes and corn are both useful and nutritious.

• Fresh fruit, fruit juice, and dried fruits—including dried apricots, dates, prunes, pears, figs, and peaches—are powerhouses of nutrients.

• Nuts and seeds are sources of concentrated goodness, too, and their link with good health has been shown in numerous studies. Yes, they are high in calories and fat, but it is mainly monounsaturated, a type of fat that is essential to keep the body functioning properly, so don't avoid them on account of their fat content.

• The "right kind of fat": I recommend the use of extra virgin olive oil for salad dressings and cooking, and a little unsalted butter at the table and for some cooking. I also use a little toasted sesame oil for flavor in some Asian dishes. I think most margarines are best avoided, and certainly those that include "hydrogenated" fats or oils, even if they claim to be high in polyunsaturates or to lower cholesterol. If you want to use margarine, buy a pure, non-hydrogenated vegetable margarine from a health food shop.

Fabulous phytoes...

Among the substances that many of these foods contain—and in which soy products such as bean curd and soy milk are particularly rich—are phytoestrogens. Phytoestrogens appear to have a health-giving, life-enhancing, balancing effect on the body's natural hormones. Studies have shown that populations whose diets are highest in phytoestrogens have a low incidence of hormone-related diseases—for example, breast, prostate, and uterine cancer; menstrual and menopausal problems, cardiovascular disease, and osteoporosis. While phytoestrogens can be particularly helpful to women, they are also of value to men (note the inclusion of prostate cancer among the diseases listed above).

The discovery of phytoestrogens and the subtle way in which they work to keep us healthy demonstrates the delicate balance of nutrients in natural ingredients and is a very strong reason for not over-refining or otherwise messing around with them. Our foods have evolved, along with us, over thousands of years, and I think we interfere at our peril. That is why I am very much in favor of organic food and very concerned about genetically modified organisms (GMOs) in our food.

Say no to GMOs

In recent decades a number of biotechnology companies have been very active in developing genetically modified organisms in order to increase yield and help crops resist disease and frost damage. The resulting produce may be introduced into the foods we eat, whether we want it or not. I am very wary of this trend because it seems to me to be going too far too quickly, and there do not seem to be adequate safeguards to protect us, the consumers, from potentially damaging effects on our health and that of our environment. It seems foolhardy to introduce rapid changes in the food chain at the instigation of multinational companies whose main aim is to provide profits for their shareholders. So, until we have much more information, I suggest you "Say no to GMOs."

We can fight this trend by avoiding food with genetically modified ingredients. This means scrutinizing labels carefully and contacting manufacturers when in doubt—or, of course, buying certified organic products. When you buy the latter you know that you are automatically avoiding GMOs.

Go organic

Organic fruits, vegetables, and other ingredients are free from GMOs as well as from the insecticides, fertilizers, and many other chemicals used in conventional agriculture. When I'm eating broccoli, for example, I want to know that that's all I'm eating, not a dose of some noxious chemicals as well. And, as long as it is fresh,

I don't mind if the broccoli is a funny shape or even contains the odd insect. That's a good sign in fact, as far as I'm concerned, and nothing that a wash in cold, slightly salted water won't remove—something that is not true of some of the chemicals used in agri-business, which get right into the plant. Fortunately, organic products are becoming much easier to find.

Storecupboard basics

All the recipes in this book are fairly simple but, in addition, I have described some as "storecupboard" recipes. These can be made from basic ingredients, listed below. If you keep these few essentials in stock you will be able to whip up a dish on the spur of the moment:

beans (canned cannellini or butter beans, red kidney beans, baked beans), bread, eggs, flour, garbanzos (canned), garlic, golden raisins, lemons, lentils (dried red), milk or soy milk, nuts (almonds, walnuts), olive oil, onions, pasta, peas (frozen), pepper, oats, potatoes, rice (especially arborio or carnaroli for risottos), salt, tomatoes (canned).

There are many more recipes that use just one or two ingredients in addition to the basics; these recipes become possible if you happen to have the extra ingredients in stock or if a quick visit to the supermarket or grocery store is practical before you cook.

A few flavorings increase the scope of your storecupboard, and once you have bought them, they're there and you don't have to think about them again. Here is a list of the ones I wouldn't like to be without:

chili powder or cayenne pepper, coriander (ground), cumin (ground), dried porcini mushrooms (especially useful for risottos), Dijon mustard, nutmeg (whole nutmegs, freshly grated, are best, but ground will do), sesame oil, soy sauce (such as tamari—see page 140), turmeric, vanilla extract.

The Shopping notes beginning on page 136 give more information on ingredients, including the less common ones used in this book.

I do hope you will enjoy using *Vegetarian Express* and that it brings you health, vitality, and more time on your hands.

Rose Elliot

fresh start breakfasts

Fresh start breakfasts

Nutritionists believe that breakfast is important and can set you up for the day; natural health practitioners have always stressed the importance of this meal and advocate that the healthy way of eating is to have the breakfast of a king, the lunch of a prince, and the evening meal of a pauper. At first, this doesn't seem to coincide with the pace at which most of us lead our lives and the number of things that have to be fitted into the morning rush.

However, a good, healthy breakfast does not take long once you are organized. Porridge takes about 7 minutes to make from start to finish, is warming and soothing, delivers a plentiful whack of vital nutrients, and is guaranteed to keep hunger pangs at bay until lunchtime. A bowl of organic muesli with nuts and dried fruit supplies the nutrients in a different form and is refreshing in warmer weather.

Also included in this section are some cooked breakfasts for when you have a little more time to spare and, at the other end of the scale, some nutritious drinks that you can whiz up and drink as you go!

Quick and creamy oatmeal with golden raisins and almonds

serves 2

calorie count 300kcal; fat content 8g per serving

scant 1 cup quick-cooking oats, preferably organic

1¼ cups calcium-enriched soy milk

1¼ cups water

⅓ cup golden raisins

1 tablespoon slivered almonds

This oatmeal tastes much creamier than its modest ingredients might suggest. I think it is the soy milk that does it—although soy milk has fewer calories than skim milk.

As well as staving off hunger pangs by keeping blood sugar levels steady for a long period, oats appear to have a normalizing effect on blood pressure when eaten regularly.

Put the oats into a saucepan—non-stick, if you have one, makes cleaning up easier—with the soy milk, water, and golden raisins. Bring to a boil, stirring, then reduce the heat and let cook gently for 5 minutes, stirring from time to time. Spoon into two bowls and serve at once, topped with the slivered almonds.

Organic maxi-muesli mix

makes about 25 servings

calorie count 250kcal;
  fat content 6g per
  2-ounce serving

1 pound organic rolled
  oats
1 pound organic jumbo
  oats or other flaked
  whole cereal grains,
  such as wheat
1⅓ cups organic raisins
  or other dried fruit,
  such as dried apricots,
  chopped dates
1 cup organic Brazil nuts,
  chopped

If you like muesli, making up your own mix gives you control over what goes into it—no whey powder, sugar, or other unwanted extras. You can ensure all the ingredients are organic and choose the ones you like. Obviously, the larger the quantity you are making up, the more you can vary the contents; on the other hand, you don't want to make up more than enough for three to four weeks at a time, otherwise the ingredients will lose their freshness.

Oats give slow-release energy, which lasts all morning; the Brazil nuts are rich in methionine, the amino acid that is often in shortest supply in the vegetarian diet. Brazil nuts are also a useful source of the trace element selenium, which helps combat free radicals (chemicals produced in the body that have been linked to cancer and many other serious health problems). I read in one newspaper that a bald man reported renewed hair growth since he started eating a bag of toffee Brazil nuts each day. It might have been something in the Brazil nuts! You might like to add some pumpkin seeds to the basic mix too, since naturopaths advocate eating some of these every day to help men ward off prostate problems and women maintain a healthy hormone balance.

Mix all the ingredients together in a large bowl, then store in a jar or other fairly airtight container, or in a polythene bag or container in the freezer, ready for use as required.

Overnight muesli

serves 1

calorie count 190kcal; fat content 4g per serving

1 rounded tablespoon organic oat flakes

1 tablespoon sweetened low-fat condensed milk

3 tablespoons cold water

1 tablespoon lemon juice and a little grated rind if you like

1 large apple or 7 ounces other fruit, such as strawberries

1 tablespoon grated hazelnuts

Very different from the previous recipe, or indeed from what we think of as muesli, Dr Bircher-Benner's original muesli was an overnight affair involving condensed milk. To be precise, I think he soaked it during the day, because he used to serve it to patients at his clinic in Switzerland for their evening meal, with thinly sliced whole wheat bread, honey, and herb tea, which I have always thought rather appealing. The condensed milk gives the muesli an attractive texture, almost slightly jellied, and it is fruit-rich rather than predominantly cereal.

The combination of oats, fruit, and nuts is rich in soluble fiber, vitamin C, magnesium, and boron: the two minerals are good for the bones and help protect against osteoporosis.

If you are using organic hazelnuts still in their brown outer skins, you might like to roast them in a moderate oven, 350°F, for 15–20 minutes until the nut kernels are golden brown. Leave the outer skins on, or rub them off in a soft cloth if you prefer.

Put the oat flakes into a cereal bowl with the condensed milk, water, lemon juice, and rind, if using, and mix. Leave overnight in the fridge or at room temperature.

In the morning, grate in the apple—skin, core, and all, according to Dr Bircher-Benner—or slice and add the strawberries or other fruit, mix and top with the hazelnuts.

Iron-rich granola

serves 4

calorie count 320kcal;
  fat content 20g per
  2-ounce serving

1 ounce sesame seeds
  (the dull, browny-grey
  type)
1 ounce sunflower seeds
2 ounces shelled pistachio
  nuts
2 ounces pumpkin seeds
2 ounces rolled oats
1 tablespoon blackstrap
  molasses
1 tablespoon water

If your iron levels need a boost—statistically no more likely in vegetarians and vegans than in meat-eaters, I hasten to add—breakfast can be an ideal time to do this. To maximize your iron intake, have this with a glass of fresh orange juice or other good source of vitamin C.

This is crunchy and very more-ish. As well as being great with yogurt or milk, it's brilliant to grab and eat dry when you are on the move, or to nibble throughout the day at those times when you want to build yourself up with a real iron boost—as well as protein, calcium, B vitamins, and zinc.

Preheat the oven to 350°F.

Put all the dry ingredients into a mixing bowl with the molasses and add the water; mix to distribute the molasses and make a lumpy mixture. Spread this out on a baking sheet, keeping the lumps, and bake for 15–20 minutes, until crisp, giving it a gentle stir after 10 minutes.

Let cool on the baking sheet, then store in an airtight container. Serve with milk—preferably soy milk—or thick yogurt.

Iron-rich breakfast compote

serves 4

calorie count 240kcal
(extra 55kcal for
pistachios); fat content
0g (extra 5g for
pistachios) per serving

1 pound mixed dried
fruits, such as apricots,
figs, prunes, peaches,
raisins, dates
1 tablespoon molasses
4 tablespoons chopped
pistachio nuts (optional)

Dried fruits are packed with nutrients and are a particularly rich source of iron. So, for a daily fix of iron, this compote takes some beating. It will keep in the fridge for several days. The molasses has a slightly smoky, toffee-ish flavor and is included to increase the iron, but you could leave it out if this isn't your priority. A sprinkling of chopped pistachios is a convenient option now that you can buy them out of their shells; it gives a pleasant crunchiness and also increases the iron content, as does a sprinkling of wheatgerm.

If you really want to boost your iron intake, you can eat this as a snack throughout the day. Besides iron, this also includes calcium, beta-carotene, riboflavin, and vitamin B6—a nutritionist's dream!

Wash the dried fruit and place it in a large mixing bowl. Dissolve the molasses in enough hot water to cover the fruit and pour over. Let soak for several hours—ideally make it in the evening to serve for breakfast the following day.

Top each serving with 1 tablespoon of chopped pistachio nuts and serve with a spoonful of Greek or other yogurt if liked.

Breakfast fruit salad

serves 4

calorie count approx
120kcal; fat content
0g per serving

1 ripe mango

6 ounces sweet seedless
grapes

4 ounces strawberries

2 kiwi fruits

1 ruby grapefruit or
2 sweet oranges

2 passion fruit

a little clear honey or
maple syrup to taste
(optional)

A refreshing fruit salad—or just some ripe fruit—is often what I fancy most for breakfast. If it is just for me, I may use only one type of fruit: luscious mango is my favorite, or sweet juicy black cherries, or mellow Cox or russet apples in the winter. If other people are sharing this feast the fruit can be more varied. For flavor as well as color include strawberries, blueberries, raspberries, watermelon, or honeydew melon in late summer when they are reliably sweet. The pulp from two or three passion fruit adds an exotic flavor. Some jewel-bright pomegranate seeds are decorative, as are sliced star fruit and physalis, with their papery sepals pulled back to reveal the orange fruits within. Serve just as it is, or with thick natural yogurt.

Packed with vitamins and minerals, including potassium, beta-carotene, and vitamin C, for a bright start to the day.

Peel the mango, then slice it. To do this, stand the mango on its end and cut down about ¼ inch either side of where the stem was. As you cut down, you will feel the hard flat stone against the knife, and you will be left with two almost halves and the central stone section. Cut away as much flesh as you can from around the stone and put it in a bowl; slice the two halves into the bowl.

Halve the grapes, hull and slice the strawberries, peel and slice the kiwi fruits and add them all to the bowl containing the mango. Hold the grapefruit over the bowl and cut away the skin, along with the pith, to reveal the juicy ruby flesh. Cut each segment away from the translucent skin around it, letting the segments and juice fall into the bowl. Cut the oranges in the same way if you are using these instead.

Cut the passion fruit in half, scoop out the seedy pulp, and add to the bowl. Give it a stir, add some honey or maple syrup to taste, if you wish, and serve.

Rosti and beans

serves 2

calorie count 290kcal; fat content 5g per serving

1 pound organic potatoes, scrubbed but not peeled

1 teaspoon fennel, caraway, or cumin seeds (optional)

salt and freshly ground black pepper

2 teaspoons olive oil

14-ounce can baked beans

A quick storecupboard cooked breakfast, this is very nutritious and filling. It is also useful for a quick supper dish or snack at any time. Very little oil is needed to make this glorious, crisp, golden brown disc of potato if you use a large non-stick skillet. Broiled tomatoes and mushrooms are excellent accompaniments, if your storecupboard can rise to them.

The beans and the potatoes are both high in complex carbohydrates, which provide lasting energy, plus vitamin C, B6, iron, and potassium.

Grate the potatoes coarsely by hand or using a food processor. Add the seeds, if using, and season well with salt and pepper.

Heat 1 teaspoon of the oil in a large skillet, preferably non-stick, and add the grated potato mixture, spreading it evenly over the base of the pan and pressing it down. Cover and cook gently for about 5 minutes, or until the underside is golden brown and crisp.

Ease the rosti away from the skillet using a fish slice or palette knife and slide it out on to a large plate. Invert another plate over it and turn the plates over, so that the rosti is now cooked-side up on the second plate. Heat the rest of the oil in the skillet, then slide the rosti off the plate into the hot oil to cook the second side. Cook, uncovered—to keep the cooked side crisp—for a further 4–5 minutes, or until the second side is golden brown and the potato is cooked right through.

A few minutes before the rosti is ready, heat the baked beans gently in a saucepan. Cut the rosti into halves or wedges and serve with the beans.

Zucchini bean curd omelet

serves 2

calorie count 200kcal; fat
content 13g per serving

1 small zucchini

1–2 teaspoons toasted
sesame oil or olive oil

8–10-ounce package of
plain bean curd

2 tablespoons soy sauce

¼ teaspoon turmeric

1 tablespoon snipped
fresh chives

salt and freshly ground
black pepper

This is not only for breakfast; it also makes a very good lunch or supper dish and you can vary it by using different vegetables; instead of zucchini, try 1 cup button mushrooms or 6–8 scallions.

Bean curd is rich in protein, iron, calcium, and phytoestrogens, which have a protective effect against a host of diseases (see page 8).

Cut the zucchini into thin slices—about ⅛ inch thick. Heat 1 teaspoon oil in a skillet, preferably non-stick, and add the zucchini slices in a single layer. Let cook over low heat while you attend to the bean curd.

Drain the bean curd, break or cut it into chunks, and place in a food processor with the soy sauce, turmeric, chives, and some freshly ground pepper. Whiz to a thick, creamy consistency. Taste, and add a little salt if necessary.

Turn the zucchini slices over, then pour and spread the bean curd mixture over the top of them. The base will brown and set, but will tend to stick to the bottom of the pan, so you will need to ease it away gently with a fish slice as it cooks. Once the base is done, flip one half of the omelet over the other in the pan. Carefully lift it out, cut in half, and serve.

Little buttermilk pancakes with blueberries

serves 4

calorie count 180kcal; fat content 8g per serving

8 ounces blueberries

1 tablespoon maple syrup or clear honey, plus extra to serve

thick Greek yogurt to serve (optional)

for the pancakes

¾ cup self-rising flour

¼ teaspoon baking soda

1 teaspoon sugar

1 egg

1¼ cups buttermilk

a little vegetable oil for frying

These make a nice breakfast or brunch treat—light, fluffy pancakes that can be whisked up in an instant and served with honey or maple syrup and melted salty organic butter, or with luscious fruit like these juicy blueberries.

Prepare the blueberries by putting them into a saucepan with the maple syrup or honey and heating gently for a few minutes, until the juices start to run. Transfer to a serving dish.

To make the pancakes, sift the flour and baking soda into a bowl and mix in the sugar. In another bowl, whisk the egg with the buttermilk, then add this to the flour, and beat to make a thick batter.

Very lightly oil a heavy-bottomed skillet—it only needs to be greased, so pour off any excess into a cup. Heat until the skillet is hot but not smoking, then drop tablespoons of the batter into the skillet, leaving a little space for them to spread.

Cook them for 1–2 minutes, until holes start to form on the surface, then flip them over and cook the other side. When the second side is set and lightly browned—this only takes about 30 seconds—lift them out of the skillet on to a warm plate. Serve at once with the blueberries, extra honey, and yogurt.

Banana smoothie

makes 1 large glass

calorie count 170kcal;
    fat content 4g

If you have time to freeze the pieces of banana this becomes thick, like an ice-cream shake. This is a real "health drink"—soothing, sustaining, rich in vitamin C, B6, folic acid, potassium, and other minerals.

1 banana

scant 1 cup vanilla soy
    milk or rice drink

1 teaspoon pure vanilla
    extract (optional)

Peel the banana and cut it into ½-inch pieces. If you have time, place them on a baking sheet and put in the freezer until frozen solid— about 1 hour. Place the banana pieces, frozen or not, into a blender or food processor with the soy milk or rice drink and the vanilla, if using. Whiz until thick and creamy; serve at once.

Variation: Mango smoothie
Cut 4 ounces peeled fresh mango or canned mango into chunks. If you have time, freeze as above. Blend with 1 cup soy milk and ¼ teaspoon ground cardamom, and serve at once.

Variation: Strawberry smoothie
Instead of the banana, begin with 4 ounces strawberries. Hull them and, if you have time, freeze as above. Blend with 1 cup soy milk and 1 teaspoon honey, and serve at once.

Pumping iron juice

makes 1 large glass

calorie count 50kcal;
    fat content 0g

You need a juicer for this recipe, but it makes a marvelous tonic, because it is rich in both iron and vitamin C, among many other vitamins and minerals. The parsley is quite strong tasting, so start with the lower quantity and add more if you like the flavor. Two glasses of this juice, made with the full quantity of parsley, supply more than the whole of the day's recommended allowance of iron.

1 pound organic carrots,
    washed

1½– 4 ounces parsley,
    washed

Cut the carrots as necessary to fit into your juicer, then push them and the parsley through the juicer. Drink as soon as possible.

Iced almond milk
with cardamom and rose water

makes 1 large glass
calorie count 370kcal;
   fat content 26g

½ cup ground almonds
1 cup ice-cold water
¼ teaspoon ground
   cardamom
½ teaspoon rose water
1 tablespoon clear honey
   or maple syrup

*A fragrant and unusual drink for when you want a "meal in a glass",
this is rich in nutrients, including iron, calcium, potassium, and B vitamins.
Although it is quite high in fat, most of this is monounsaturated—a type
of fat that has been shown to lower blood cholesterol levels.*

Place all the ingredients in a blender or food processor. Whiz
together, pour into a glass, and serve at once.

Pineapple and apricot reviver

makes 1 large glass
calorie count 320kcal;
   fat content 2g

1¼ cups pineapple juice
6 ready-to-eat dried
   apricots
1 tablespoon yeast flakes
1 tablespoon wheatgerm
4 ice cubes

*Both a pick-me-up—because of the vitamin C—and a meal in a glass,
rich in iron, potassium, and B vitamins.*

Put all the ingredients into a blender or food processor and whiz
very thoroughly to purée the apricots as much as possible. Pour
into a glass and serve at once.

*vitality-boosting
lunches*

Speedy soups

High-vitality foods provide a natural pick-me-up and can be made into speedy soups for a warming lunch, either on their own or with bread and cheese, sandwiches, or salad.

Homemade stock is wonderful, of course, but lack of stock is no reason for not making soup. Water is fine if you are using well-flavored ingredients. Alternatively, you could use a good stock powder—Marigold vegetable bouillon, from health food shops and some supermarkets, is my favorite—or you can use my lazy stock method. For this you simply cook stock ingredients—a carrot, piece of onion, celery stalk, any herbs you happen to have—in your pot of soup and scoop them out before you blend the soup. You could also blend these flavorings with the soup if they would enhance it.

Quick pea soup

serves 2–3

calorie count 155–230 kcal; fat content 6–8g per serving

1 small onion, finely chopped
1 tablespoon olive oil
8 ounces peeled and diced potatoes
1⅔ cups frozen petits pois
3 cups water or vegetable stock
6 sprigs of mint
salt and freshly ground black pepper
1 tablespoon roughly chopped fresh mint to garnish

This is a great storecupboard recipe if you keep a package of frozen peas in the freezer—and forget about the mint unless you have some handy. In any case, this is a very quick soup. You could make it even quicker simply by cooking the peas a little then blending them; however, the onion and potato base gives more flavor and a creamier texture.

Peas are powerhouses of nutrients. This soup is rich in folic acid, vitamin C, thiamin, and iron, and also contains useful amounts of beta-carotene, zinc, and protein.

Fry the onion in the oil in a large saucepan for 5 minutes, or until softened but not browned. Add the diced potatoes, stir, and cook for a further 5 minutes. Add the frozen peas, water or stock, and mint sprigs. Bring to a boil, then simmer gently for 15 minutes or until the potatoes are tender.

Remove the mint sprigs, then whiz the soup in a blender or food processor. Season to taste and serve garnished with the chopped fresh mint.

The most comforting soup in the world

makes 4 large servings

calorie count 210kcal; fat
content 4g per serving

1 tablespoon olive oil

1 pound onions, sliced

1½ pounds potatoes,
    peeled and cut into
    ½-inch pieces

5 cups water

freshly grated nutmeg

salt and freshly ground
    black pepper

Everyone has their favorite comfort foods that they turn to when the going gets tough, and this is one of mine. It's soothing when you have a cold or feel unwell; it is also uplifting when you are feeling low. It's quick and easy to make from the most basic storecupboard ingredients, so don't be put off by the rather unusual method involving two saucepans.

High in carbohydrates for steady energy, plus iron, protein, vitamin B6, potassium, vitamin C, and flavonoids to keep blood and arteries healthy.

Heat the olive oil in a saucepan. Add the onions, cover the pan, and cook very gently until the onions are really tender but not browned; about 15–20 minutes.

Meanwhile, put the potatoes in another saucepan with the water. Bring to a boil and cook until very tender. Then put the potatoes with their cooking water and a big spoonful of the cooked onion into a blender or food processor and blend to a smooth cream.

Mix this potato cream with the remaining onions, adding a little more water if necessary to give the consistency you want. Season to taste with plenty of freshly grated nutmeg, salt, and pepper. Reheat gently and serve.

Oven-baked sweet potato and red pepper soup

serves 4

calorie count 150kcal; fat content 4g per serving

1 pound yellow-fleshed sweet potatoes, peeled and diced

1 red onion, roughly sliced

1 tablespoon vegetable oil

2 red bell peppers, halved and deseeded

1¾–2¼ cups vegetable stock

salt and freshly ground black pepper

paprika to garnish

This isn't an instant soup because you do have to allow time—about 45 minutes—for the vegetables to bake in the oven. However, the preparation is so effortless and the soup so good that I felt it had a place in this book. Of course, if you are organized to do the baking part in advance—perhaps the day before when the oven is on for something else—then the soup practically makes itself.

Rich in beta-carotene for healthy eyes, hair, nails, lungs, and throat, and increased resistance to infection.

Preheat the oven to 400°F. Put the sweet potatoes and onion in a roasting pan, sprinkle with the oil, and move them around with your hands to distribute the oil. Add the peppers, then bake until all the vegetables are tender—about 45 minutes.

Place the cooked vegetables in a blender or food processor with some of the stock and blend until smooth. Add more stock a little at a time and blend after each addition, until you have the consistency you want. Tip the soup into a saucepan, season with salt and pepper to taste, and reheat before serving, sprinkled with paprika.

If you are making the soup as soon as the vegetables are cooked, and want to eat it immediately, have the stock already hot, then you won't have to reheat the soup in a saucepan after you have blended it.

Variations

Stir a pat of creamed coconut into the soup after blending. It will melt as the soup is reheated, giving it a creamy sweetness which may need a squeeze of lemon or lime juice to balance it.

Another option is to make the soup hotter by adding a little cayenne pepper or chili powder.

Quick lentil soup

serves 4

calorie count 270kcal; fat content 5g per serving

1 onion, finely chopped

1 tablespoon olive oil

1 cup split red lentils

4 cups water

1 carrot

1 celery stalk

lemon juice to taste

salt and coarsely ground black pepper

optional flavorings

1 tablespoon grated fresh gingerroot

1–2 teaspoons ground coriander

1–2 teaspoons ground cumin

½ teaspoon turmeric

Lentil soup is one of the quickest and easiest soups to make, and it is so versatile. You can make it thick and filling so that you can almost stand a spoon up in it, or thin and smooth enough to drink from a large mug, which is exactly what I'm doing as I write—and very warming and comforting it is, too. I have flavored it with lemon juice and crushed garlic but often I will warm it up with curry spices: ground cumin, coriander, a pinch of turmeric, a few crushed cardamoms, maybe a hint of chili, although I don't like it too throat-raspingly hot. For a sweet, luxurious version, when you don't mind about the calories, stir a pat of creamed coconut, cut from a block, into the hot thick soup.

Leftover lentil soup makes a tasty dhal-like sauce for steamed, broiled or roasted vegetables. If there's lots over and it is thick, thicken it even more with bread crumbs or matzo meal, so it is just firm enough to shape into little patties. Shallow-fry them in a little olive oil until crisp on both sides and serve at once with natural yogurt flavored with chopped herbs or scallion, and a salad or cooked green vegetable.

Wonderfully nutritious: high in protein and complex carbohydrates, and also in folic acid, iron, thiamin, vitamin B6, and zinc.

Fry the onion in the oil in a large saucepan for 5 minutes, until beginning to soften. Then add the lentils and water, and the carrot and celery, which are for flavoring. Bring to a boil and simmer for 20 minutes, or until the lentils are tender. Add any combination of the optional flavorings and simmer for a further 4–5 minutes.

You can leave the soup as it is, or purée it in a blender or food processor for a smooth texture—removing the carrot and celery first, or leaving them in, as you prefer. Adjust the consistency with more water if necessary. Add a squeeze of lemon juice, and salt and pepper to taste. Serve with a grinding of black pepper over the top.

Udon noodles in ginger miso broth

serves 4

calorie count 50gkcal; fat
content 4g per serving

1 leek, cleaned and cut
into ¼-inch slices

1 tablespoon toasted
sesame oil

2 tablespoons grated
fresh gingerroot

1–2 bok choy (pak choi)
or 4 ounces tender
spinach leaves,
washed and chopped

4 cups water or
vegetable stock

4 tablespoons tamari
or other soy sauce

7 ounces fresh or vacuum-
packed udon noodles

1 tablespoon miso

salt

A quick and filling Japanese-style soup. You can buy vacuum packs of the noodles in large supermarkets or in Chinese or Japanese food shops, which will also have the bok choy, sometimes known as pak choi, although you can use spinach instead. A supermarket may also have the miso—or you will certainly get it in a health food shop. There are various types (see page 137); it will keep for months in the fridge.

Fry the leek gently in the oil in a large saucepan for about 10 minutes, until softened but not browned. Then stir in the ginger and cook for 1–2 minutes. Add the bok choy or spinach, stirring it a few times as it softens and wilts in the heat. Once this has happened—after about 5 minutes—pour in the water or stock and tamari and bring to a boil.

Add the noodles and simmer for about 3 minutes, until cooked; remove from the heat, stir in the miso and salt to taste, then serve.

Spinach soup

serves 2–3

calorie count 140–200
   kcal; fat content 5–8g
   per serving

1 small onion, finely
   chopped

1 tablespoon olive oil

8 ounces peeled and
   diced potatoes

8 ounces tender spinach
   leaves, washed

3 cups water or
   vegetable stock

freshly grated nutmeg

salt and freshly ground
   black pepper

Ready-washed spinach can be quickly made into a glorious green soup. You could also use frozen spinach, so if you keep a package in the freezer this is a potential "storecupboard" soup.

Spinach has been found by many scientific studies to greatly reduce the risk of strokes and heart attacks.

Fry the onion in the oil in a large saucepan for 5 minutes, or until softened but not browned. Then add the potatoes, stir, and cook for a further 5 minutes.

Add the spinach, pressing it down well, and stirring it a few times as it softens and wilts in the heat. Once this has happened—after about 5 minutes—pour in the water or stock, bring to a boil, then simmer gently for 10–15 minutes, until the potatoes are tender. Purée the soup in a blender or food processor, reheat, and season to taste with freshly grated nutmeg, salt, and pepper.

Mediterranean split pea soup

serves 2

calorie count 340kcal; fat content 2g per serving (excluding olive oil added at the table)

1 cup yellow or green split peas

5 cups water or vegetable stock

1 large onion, chopped

salt and freshly ground black pepper

to serve

1 large sweet mild onion, sliced

extra virgin olive oil

It is the contrast between the soft, sweetish golden mash of split peas, the juicy crunch of the raw onions, and the thick green olive oil, slathered over the top, which makes this so good. Although this takes about 1 hour to cook, it takes only moments to prepare and therefore qualifies as an "express" dish. Serve with chunks of good bread.

Packed with nutrients: protein, folic acid, iron, and thiamin, as well as slow-release energy from the complex carbohydrates.

Put the split peas into a saucepan with the water or stock and the chopped onion. Bring to a boil, then simmer for 45–60 minutes, or until the peas are very tender and mushy. Check the consistency, adding some more water or stock if necessary, but keeping the soup thick. Season to taste with salt and pepper.

Serve in warmed bowls, top with raw mild onion and olive oil and serve with plenty of bread.

Dips and dressings

These dips and dressings are creamy yet not high in fat or calories. They are excellent for dipping raw vegetables into, for serving with salad, or—to make them into more of a meal—with broiled, roasted, or steamed vegetables, and of course with baked potatoes.

A couple of them—Ricotta "mayonnaise" and Quick creamy mustard dressing—make fast, low-fat alternatives to mayonnaise when you want to save some calories as well as time. They are great in sandwiches or for dipping, as is creamy Hummus (see page 40).

Gomasio isn't really a dip, just a tasty seasoning that seemed to fit into this section, especially as it is delicious with raw vegetables—just dip them in and eat. It's salty and a bit oily, but low in sodium and certainly not packed with fat—just flavorsome and healthy.

Ricotta "mayonnaise"

serves 4

calorie count 40kcal; fat content 3g per serving

2 ounces ricotta cheese
2 ounces quark cheese
2 teaspoons olive oil
½ teaspoon white wine vinegar

Although this does not have the flavor or the delicate, wobbly texture of mayonnaise, it is creamy and piquant and does make quite a decent substitute in certain dishes—some sandwiches, for instance—at a fraction of the calories and fat content.

Quite low in fat and rich in calcium, protein, and riboflavin.

Combine all the ingredients by whisking together in a bowl or whizzing them in a food processor until smooth and light.

Quick creamy mustard dressing

serves 2–4

calorie count 25kcal;
fat content 2g per
tablespoon

6 tablespoons soy cream
(see page 140)
1 tablespoon Dijon
mustard
1 tablespoon white wine
or cider vinegar
salt and freshly ground
black pepper

This dressing is useful when you fancy something that tastes rich and creamy but is not too high in fat and calories. I love it as a dip for raw vegetables or poured over crunchy raw salad mixtures, such as shredded cabbage and grated carrot. It is also good over drained canned beans.

A source of valuable phytoestrogens (see page 8).

Place all the ingredients in a small bowl and mix together—the vinegar has a slightly thickening effect on the cream. Season to taste.

Gomasio

Makes 6 teaspoons

calorie count 15kcal;
fat content 1g per
teaspoon

1 ounce grey/brown (not
white) sesame seeds
1 teaspoon good-quality
sea salt

This mixture is frequently used as a seasoning in Japanese cooking It is good sprinkled over all kinds of dishes or just served with vegetable crudités and olive oil, dipping them first in the oil, then in the gomasio.

Using this as a condiment may help you to cut down on the amount of salt you use. Sesame seeds are rich in nutrients, containing iron and zinc, even though this is used in small quantities.

Put the sesame seeds and salt into a small saucepan and stir over moderate heat for 1–2 minutes, until the toasted seeds smell aromatic and start to jump out of the pan. Let cool slightly, then grind to powder using a coffee grinder or a pestle and mortar. This keeps well in a screw-top jar in the fridge for up to 4 weeks.

Quick cannellini bean pâté

serves 2–4

calorie count 90–170kcal; fat content 4–8g per serving

8-ounce can cannellini beans

1–2 garlic cloves, peeled

1 tablespoon lemon juice

1 tablespoon olive oil

1 teaspoon red wine vinegar or cider vinegar

1 tablespoon chopped fresh herbs or scallion (optional)

salt and black pepper

Useful as a sandwich filling (see page 47), as an appetizer or snack, perhaps with some crisp Melba toast, or served as a salad, with sliced tomatoes, black olives, and whatever salad leaves are available. I also like it as a creamy, protein-rich sauce with broiled or roasted vegetables.

Filling and sustaining because of the complex carbohydrates, this is also rich in protein, iron, potassium, thiamin, and folic acid.

Drain the beans and reserve the liquid. Put the beans in a food processor with the whole garlic cloves, lemon juice, olive oil, and vinegar. Whiz thoroughly to make a smooth purée. It will be very thick, so add 1–2 tablespoons of the reserved liquid from the canned beans to thin it to the consistency you want. Add the fresh herbs or scallion, if using, and season to taste with salt and pepper.

Golden pepper sauce

serves 4

calorie count 25kcal; fat content 0.1g per serving

1 large yellow bell pepper, deseeded and chopped

1 garlic clove, sliced or chopped

1 teaspoon red or white wine vinegar

4 ounces quark cheese

salt and freshly ground black pepper

A smooth and creamy, yet virtually fat-free, buttercup-colored sauce for serving with raw or cooked vegetables.

Yellow bell peppers are rich in beta-carotene; the quark provides calcium and protein.

Put the chopped pepper into a small saucepan. Add water to a depth of about ½ inch and bring to a boil. Cover and cook gently for 10–15 minutes, until the pepper is very tender. Drain, then put the chunks of pepper and the garlic into a blender or food processor and blend until smooth. Add the vinegar and quark and blend again. Season to taste with salt and pepper.

Top to bottom: Quick cannellini bean pâté; Spicy hummus; Golden pepper sauce

Spicy hummus

serves 4

calorie count 240kcal; fat
content 14g per serving

14-ounce can garbanzos
(chickpeas)

1–2 garlic cloves, peeled

½ cup lemon juice
(juice from 1 large
or 2 small lemons)

4 tablespoons tahini

1 tablespoon cumin seeds

a good pinch of chili
powder

salt

to serve

lemon wedges

black olives

paprika

An old friend with a bit of a new twist, and such a useful recipe that I felt it had to be included. I am surprised how few people make their own hummus. If you have a food processor, it is easier to whiz up a batch of hummus at home than it is to wait in the line at the deli, and this tastes better than any hummus that you can buy. I wouldn't describe this as a "storecupboard" recipe because you could hardly call tahini an everyday storecupboard item, although it keeps for ages. However, if you do keep a jar in stock, along with a can of garbanzos, some lemons, and garlic, you'll never be stuck for a healthy and sustaining snack, not to mention appetizer, dip or sandwich filling.

Extremely nutritious, almost a "wonder food" really, since it is packed with iron, folic acid, zinc, protein, and copious calcium.

Drain the garbanzos and reserve the liquid. Put the garbanzos into a food processor with the whole garlic cloves, lemon juice, and tahini. Blend thoroughly until smooth. The mixture will be very thick, so add 2–3 tablespoons of the reserved liquid from the canned garbanzos to thin it down—the exact amount will depend on how thick the tahini was.

Toast the cumin seeds by stirring them over gentle heat in a dry saucepan for a minute or so until they smell aromatic and begin to pop. Stir into the hummus along with the chili powder; season with salt to taste.

To serve as a dip, I usually spread the hummus out over a plate so that it is about ½ inch thick, surround it with thick lemon wedges and juicy black olives, and sprinkle it with mild paprika. Another option is to sprinkle the top with Gomasio (see page 37), for additional sesame flavor.

Sexy sandwiches

Yes, sandwiches are sexy, or they can be, but you have to get everything right—fresh, tasty bread packed with a delectable moist filling that is impossible to eat neatly or tidily. Sandwiches need to be generous, which puts me in mind of the saying "cooking, like love, has to be entered into with abandon or not at all." Even so, they don't have to be ridiculously high in calories and fat, as the following recipes prove.

Have a look at the breads in your local bakery or supermarket, because the range seems to expand almost weekly. One way of enjoying variety is to buy several, get them sliced or slice them yourself, and store them in the freezer. Then you can take a couple of slices of whatever takes your fancy when you want to make a sandwich.

I have suggested some breads that go well with the fillings but there are plenty of others, so feel free to mix and match, and to use breads that I haven't mentioned. The flavored flat breads from California, which you spread with the filling and then fold up like a parcel, for instance, make an interesting change and are fairly tidy to eat.

Avocado and arugula on sesame bread

serves 1

calorie count approx
300kcal; fat content
approx 13g

Spread a slice of sesame or whole-grain bread with 1–1½ ounces smooth soft white cheese or goat cheese, low or medium fat as you prefer. Lay slices of ripe avocado on top, using ½ a small avocado per sandwich. Cover with fresh arugula leaves and season with salt and freshly ground black pepper. Spread another slice of bread with soft cheese and press on top.

Hummus, black olives and cilantro on granary

serves 1

calorie count approx
250kcal; fat content
approx 6g

Spread two slices of whole-grain bread with hummus (see page 40), allowing 1–1½ ounces per sandwich, and top with pitted and sliced black olives, and cilantro leaves.

Alternatively, spread one slice of bread with black olive pâté and the other with hummus and sandwich the cilantro leaves in between.

Cream cheese, date, and mint on walnut bread

serves 1

calorie count approx
200kcal; fat content
approx 1g

Spread a slice of walnut bread with 1½ ounces smooth white creamy cheese or goat cheese. Top with 2 large pitted and sliced fresh dates and some chopped fresh mint.

Left to right: Avocado and arugula; Hummus, black olive and cilantro; Cream cheese, date and mint

Peanut butter or tahini with grated carrot and bean sprouts on whole-grain

serves 1

calorie count 500kcal;
fat content approx 28g

This has an old-fashioned feel about it—certainly for me, as these were the sandwiches I used to have in my school lunch box—but it is actually a pretty good mixture if you fancy something salady and nutty with loads of vitamins.

Spread two slices of whole-grain bread with peanut butter or tahini. If it is difficult to spread, soften it with a few drops of hot water. Top one slice with some grated carrot and bean sprouts or alfalfa, then press the other slice on top. Watercress is another option, or some sliced tomato and chopped scallion if you are going to eat the sandwich almost immediately.

Brie and fruit chutney on whole-grain

serves 1

calorie count 300kcal;
fat content approx 12g

If several types of Brie are available, it's worth reading the nutritional label: some types may be lower in fat than others.

If you make this with gloriously ripe, runny Brie, you can spread it, including the rind, on the slices of bread, allowing 2 ounces for each sandwich. Spoon 1 tablespoon sweet and spicy peach, apricot, or mango chutney on top and press the slices of bread together.

Instead of Brie you can use grated vegan cheese; you will need to spread the bread with pure vegetable margarine and use plenty of chutney.

Broiled asparagus and goat cheese on light rye

serves 1

calorie count 250kcal;
fat content approx 4g

The fine, ready-trimmed asparagus sold in supermarkets is ideal for this. Allow about 5–6 small spears for each sandwich. Brush the trimmed asparagus very lightly with a mixture of half olive oil, half lemon juice, or use an oil-and-water spray (see page 138). Cook the spears under a preheated hot broiler until the asparagus is tinged with brown and just tender. Let cool.

Spread two slices of light rye bread with 1–1½ ounces smooth mild goat cheese, then sandwich the asparagus between them.

Date spread and crushed pistachios on mixed-grain bread

serves 1

calorie count 400kcal;
fat content approx 5g

Make the date spread by gently heating ⅓ cup chopped dates with 1 tablespoon water until soft, then beat until smooth and let cool. Add 1 tablespoon chopped pistachio nuts or pumpkin seeds. Spread this over two slices of mixed-grain bread and press together.

Luxurious vegan salad sandwich on sunflower-seed bread

serves 1

calorie count 300kcal;

fat content approx 10g

Luxurious and vegan are not words that you often see together, although vegan food can be very luxurious, not to say downright decadent. Olive oil, coconut cream, good-quality chocolate, avocado, the full range of nuts and their oils, truffles, saffron, and vintage Champagne are all vegan— but I digress. Anyway, this is a luxurious sandwich and it is vegan. You do need to shop carefully for vegan mayonnaise, or make it yourself, but once you have found it, you are away.

Spread two slices of sunflower-seed bread with vegan mayonnaise. Put some crisp lettuce leaves on top of one slice, add some slices of tomato, cucumber, and avocado, and season well with salt and freshly ground black pepper. Top with the second piece of bread and press down gently but firmly.

Vegetable pâté and cucumber on mixed-grain bread

serves 1

calorie count 250kcal;

fat content approx 6g

These sandwiches need to be eaten fairly soon after making them, otherwise the cucumber makes them a bit soggy. If you are not eating them immediately, use some shredded Little Gem lettuce instead or vitamin C-rich mustard and cress or salad cress.

Spread two slices of mixed-grain bread fairly thickly with 1½–2 ounces vegetable pâté (Tartex Swiss vegetable pâté is a long-time favorite in my family and is available from health food shops). Cover with thinly sliced cucumber, season with salt and freshly ground black pepper, then press together.

Broiled pepper and onion with basil on garlic bread

serves 1

calorie count 230kcal;

fat content approx 4g

Allow ½ red bell pepper and ½ small red onion per sandwich. Cut the onion into thick slices, lightly brush with oil or use an oil-and-water spray (see page 138) and place under a preheated broiler with the halved red pepper, skin-side up. Cook the pepper until charred and tender. Cook the onion until lightly browned on one side, then turn, and cook the other side. Allow the broiled vegetables to cool.

Remove the skin from the pepper if liked and cut the flesh into thin ribbons. Spread two slices of a garlic-flavored bread with soft low-fat white cheese or goat cheese, allowing 1–1½ ounces per sandwich. Top with the broiled vegetables and some fresh basil leaves and press together.

Cannellini bean pâté sandwiches

serves 1

calorie count 250kcal;

fat content approx 4g

Make the Quick cannellini bean pâté (see page 38) and spread it generously on two slices of whole-grain bread. Add whatever extra ingredients you happen to have—sweet mango or apricot chutney goes well, as does a smear of black olive pâté and, if you are going to eat the sandwiches fairly soon, slices of tomato. Chopped chives or scallions are another option, as is shredded lettuce.

Honey-roasted eggplant with sesame and hummus in pita

serves 2

calorie count 400kcal; fat
content 24g per serving

1 eggplant

1 tablespoon toasted
sesame oil

1 tablespoon balsamic
vinegar

1 tablespoon clear honey

1 tablespoon soy sauce

1 teaspoon sesame seeds

2 pita breads

4 tablespoons hummus
(see page 40)

Prepared like this, eggplant has a delectable texture that really melts in your mouth. Combine it with silky hummus for a sensual feast with a Middle Eastern flavor.

Eggplants are a rich source of natural nicotine, so can be a useful food to eat if you are giving up smoking.

Cut the eggplant into ½-inch slices, removing and discarding the stem. Mix the oil, vinegar, honey, and soy sauce together in a small bowl, then brush this over the slices of eggplant. Cook the slices under a preheated hot broiler until they are golden brown on one side, then turn them over and cook the other side. Just before they are done, sprinkle with the sesame seeds and cook for a further couple of minutes until roasted.

Open up the pita breads and spread with the hummus, then fill with the eggplant, and serve at once.

Big broiled mushroom in a bun

serves 1

calorie count 230kcal;
fat content 5g

1 large mushroom

olive or garlic oil for
brushing

salt and pepper

1 burger bun, split

This can be made in a flash—a big, juicy mushroom, broiled until tender and oozing inky liquid, then pushed inside a soft bun and eaten at once.

Brush the mushroom with oil. Place the mushroom, gills down, under a preheated broiler and cook for 3–4 minutes, until it begins to soften. Then turn it over and cook the other side until it is tender and juicy—about another 3–4 minutes. Season with salt and pepper, insert the mushroom into the burger bun, and serve at once.

Mexican tortillas with peppers and beans

serves 4

calorie count 350kcal; fat
  content 22g per serving

1 tablespoon olive oil

1 onion, chopped

1 red bell pepper,
  deseeded and chopped

2 garlic cloves,
  finely chopped

2 teaspoons cumin seeds

14-ounce can plum
  tomatoes in juice

14-ounce can red kidney
  beans, drained

salt and freshly ground
  black pepper

4 wheat tortillas

1 large ripe avocado,
  chopped

⅔ cup sour cream or
  Greek yogurt

chopped fresh cilantro

Filling, sustaining and packed with nutrients—loads of protein, iron, and B vitamins.

Heat the oil in a large flameproof casserole dish—if possible one that you can take to the table afterward—and add the onion and pepper. Cover and cook gently for 7 minutes, until tender but not browned. Add the garlic and cumin seeds and cook for another 2–3 minutes. Then add the tomatoes and cook, uncovered, for about 15 minutes, until thick. Add the drained kidney beans, heat through and season to taste with salt and pepper.

Meanwhile, warm the tortillas under a preheated broiler, in the oven, or by heating in a dry skillet for a few seconds on each side. Put the accompaniments—the chopped avocado, sour cream, and cilantro—into small bowls.

Bring the casserole containing the bean mixture, and the accompaniments, to the table. Let everyone help themselves to a warm tortilla, heap the beans on to it, then top with the avocado, sour cream, and cilantro.

Super salads

Quick, light, yet sustaining, salads are just right for lunch, to restore flagging energy, perk you up, and take you through the afternoon.

The recipes here range from the light and juicy Ruby grapefruit, green olive, and fennel salad, the quirky Onion, date, and dill and the bursting-with-nutrients Avocado and alfalfa to the more filling salads that contain ingredients such as lentils, beans, bean curd and a "tagliatelle" of omelet.

Cannellini bean salad with creamy mustard dressing

serves 2

calorie count 230kcal; fat
content 9g per serving

1 round lettuce
Quick creamy mustard
dressing (see page 37)
14-ounce can cannellini
beans, drained
3–4 scallions, chopped
or sliced
salt and freshly ground
black pepper

A salad that fills you up and gives you lasting energy, along with plenty of protein, vitamins, and minerals.

Wash the lettuce and leave to drain in a colander while you prepare the mustard dressing.

Arrange the lettuce leaves on two plates. Mix the drained beans with the scallions and a little salt and pepper. Spoon on top of the lettuce, then pour the mustard dressing over the top and serve.

Spinach, mushroom, and smoked bean curd

serves 2

calorie count 250kcal; fat
content 22g per serving

5 ounces smoked bean
curd

olive oil for frying, plus
extra for the dressing

4 ounces firm white
mushrooms

1 tablespoon balsamic
vinegar

salt and freshly ground
black pepper

4 ounces baby spinach
leaves, washed and torn

This is an unashamed copy of a non-vegetarian salad, the paper-thin, crisply fried slices of smoked bean curd standing in for crunchy shards of smoky-flavored bacon. Well, if it's a flavor and texture that works, why not a vegetarian version?

Note, if you buy a standard-sized block of bean curd there will be some left over. It will keep, wrapped in plastic wrap, for several days in the fridge; alternatively, you can freeze it.

Light to eat, yet packed with protein, iron, and other nutrients.

Cut the bean curd into narrow, paper-thin slices—the thinner they are, the crisper they'll be, which is one of the joys of this salad.

Cover the base of a skillet thinly with olive oil and heat. When it is sizzling hot, add some of the bean curd slices—they can be close together but must be in a single layer. Fry until they are really golden brown on one side, then flip them over with a palette knife and fry the other side. This may take 7–10 minutes—don't hurry them. Drain the first batch of bean curd slices on paper towels and repeat the process with the remaining bean curd until you have a golden crunchy pile.

Meanwhile, slice the mushrooms very thinly, cutting through the stem to produce paper-thin mushroom shapes. Place in a bowl with a few drops of balsamic vinegar, 1 tablespoon of olive oil, and a little salt and pepper. Mix gently, then add the torn spinach and mix again, adding a little more seasoning, vinegar, and olive oil as necessary.

Finally, add the crispy bean curd, and check again in case a touch more vinegar or seasoning are needed. Serve at once.

Avocado and alfalfa salad

serves 2

calorie count 300kcal; fat content 15g per serving

handful of alfalfa sprouts

1 large ripe avocado, peeled and sliced

2 scallions, shredded

small handful of raisins

2 tomatoes, skinned and sliced

juice of ½ lemon

Although avocados are high in fat, it is the right kind of fat, and they are packed with other nutritious goodies, too. Paired with that other vitamin-packed vegetable, alfalfa, they make an energizing salad. Because of the oil in the avocado, I tend to dress the salad lightly—using lemon juice and sliced tomatoes to add juice—but you could add 1 tablespoon of olive oil as well, if you like. You can buy alfalfa sprouts at some health food shops and supermarkets, or you can sprout them yourself (see page 136).

Mega-nutrients here—alfalfa has been called "the father of all foods" in Arabic and has been shown to lower cholesterol by absorbing it from the digestive tract. Alfalfa also contains an anti-bacterial agent, the amino acid L-canaverine, which has been shown to have anti-cancer properties.

Mix all the ingredients together in a large bowl and serve.

Ruby grapefruit, green olive, and fennel salad

serves 2

calorie count 170kcal; fat
   content 6g per serving

1 ruby grapefruit
3–4 ounces large green
   olives
1 small bulb of fennel
1 teaspoon coarsely
   crushed pepper
watercress or arugula
   leaves

Chunks of ruby grapefruit, large green olives, and paper-thin slices of fennel make a salad that is salty-sharp, sweet-sour, crisp, and juicy.

An excellent pick-me-up because of all the vitamin C, this salad also contains iron—from the olives and green leaves—and other nutrients.

Holding the grapefruit over a bowl, cut away the skin and the pith to reveal the jewel-bright, juicy flesh. Cut the segments out of their translucent skins, letting them fall into the bowl along with any juice.

Give each olive a sharp whack with the back of a wooden spoon and it will split open, allowing you to remove the pit easily. Put the smashed olives into the bowl with the grapefruit.

Remove the outermost leaves of the fennel, or just shave them with a potato peeler or sharp knife if they seem reasonably tender. Cut the fennel in half and then into paper-thin slices; add these to the bowl together with any of the leafy green fronds.

To serve, arrange the watercress or arugula on individual plates. Spoon the salad on top and grind some black pepper over it.

Asparagus and red pepper salad with cannellini cream

serves 2

calorie count 270kcal; fat
    content 8g per serving

1 lemon

1 tablespoon olive oil

8-ounce bunch of
    asparagus, trimmed
    as necessary

2 red bell peppers,
    halved and deseeded

14-ounce can cannellini
    beans, drained
    and rinsed

1 garlic clove, crushed

4 tablespoons water

1 tablespoon Dijon
    mustard

1 tablespoon balsamic
    vinegar

1 tablespoon clear honey

2 ounces baby spinach,
    washed

coarsely ground black
    pepper

Cannellini beans make a splendid purée and I love the contrast of this starchy, creamy mixture with the sweet, slightly crisp broiled vegetables.

A main course salad that is satisfying, refreshing, and rich in vitamins and minerals.

Use a zester to remove long strips of peel from the lemon. Alternatively, peel off long thin strips with a sharp knife or potato peeler, then cut into long shreds. Squeeze the juice from the lemon. Mix 1 tablespoon of the lemon juice with the olive oil and brush the asparagus with this mixture.

Place the asparagus under a preheated broiler, together with the peppers, their shiny sides up. Broil for 10–15 minutes, or until the peppers are charred and blistered in places, and the asparagus is tender and slightly flecked with brown. Remove the vegetables from the broiler and set aside. When the peppers are cool enough to handle, cut them into thick ribbons, first removing the charred skins if you like.

Place the drained beans in a food processor with the garlic, 1 tablespoon of the lemon juice, the water, and a little coarsely ground black pepper. Process until smooth and creamy.

Make a dressing by whisking together the mustard, balsamic vinegar, honey, and 1 tablespoon of the lemon juice in a small bowl, or by shaking the ingredients well in a screw-top jar.

Arrange the spinach leaves on two plates. Spoon over some of the cannellini bean cream, then layer the red pepper strips, asparagus, and remaining cannellini cream on top. Drizzle the dressing over the top, scatter with the lemon rind and black pepper, and serve at once.

Warm butter bean salad with scallions and maple mustard dressing

serves 2

calorie count 250kcal; fat
content 8g per serving

14-ounce can butter beans

2 tablespoons maple
syrup

1 tablespoon Dijon
mustard

1 tablespoon balsamic
vinegar

1 tablespoon olive oil

6 scallions, chopped

2–3 tablespoons chopped
fresh cilantro

5 ounces salad leaves

A few basic storecupboard ingredients are combined with some fresh herbs, leaves, and scallions to make a filling salad.

Soluble fiber in the beans lowers cholesterol, helps control appetite, and slows absorption of sugars.

Place the butter beans and their liquid in a saucepan and warm over a moderate heat for about 5 minutes, until heated through.

Meanwhile, mix together the maple syrup, mustard, balsamic vinegar, and olive oil in a small bowl.

Drain the beans and mix gently with the maple syrup dressing, the scallions, and the chopped cilantro. Spoon on to a base of salad leaves and serve.

Onion, date, and dill salad

serves 2

calorie count 430kcal; fat
content 20g per serving

1 mild, sweet, juicy onion,
very thinly sliced

1 tablespoon olive oil

1 drop of red wine vinegar
or squeeze of
lemon juice

salt and freshly ground
black pepper

8 ounces fresh dates

2 tablespoons fresh dill,
lightly chopped

4 ounces feta cheese,
diced

*An odd-sounding combination of ingredients, but it works. Serve with
some rye bread.*

*Very rich in potassium, this also contains useful amounts of niacin, iron,
and vitamin B6.*

Place the onion slices in a bowl and sprinkle with the olive oil, a drop
of vinegar or a squeeze of lemon juice, and some salt and pepper.

Halve the dates, remove the pits and add the dates to the onion,
along with the dill and feta cheese. Stir gently and serve.

Red lentil salad with ginger and chili

serves 2

calorie count 190kcal; fat content 8g per serving

½ cup split red lentils

1¼ cups water

1 tablespoon olive oil

1 small onion, finely chopped

1 garlic clove, crushed

1 tablespoon chopped fresh gingerroot

2 tablespoons sherry

2 tablespoons shoyu or tamari soy sauce

2 tablespoons balsamic vinegar

1 large fresh red chili pepper, halved, deseeded and finely sliced

salt and coarsely ground black pepper

4 ounces young spinach leaves, washed

torn fresh basil leaves to garnish

You can almost make this from the storecupboard ingredients listed on page 9; however, you do also need some fresh gingerroot, chili, and a few flavorings, which might not be to hand, and of course the tender young spinach leaves to serve with it. It's a lovely salad and easy to make.

Filling, low in fat, and high in iron, protein, and complex carbohydrates.

Place the lentils and water in a saucepan and cook for 15–20 minutes, until the lentils are tender but not broken and the water has been absorbed. Drain away any water that remains.

Meanwhile, heat the oil in a large saucepan, add the onion and fry for about 7 minutes, until nearly tender and flecked with brown. Add the garlic, ginger, sherry, shoyu or tamari, balsamic vinegar, and chili and let the mixture bubble until half of the liquid has evaporated and the mixture looks syrupy.

Mix the drained cooked lentils with the onion mixture, and season to taste with salt and plenty of coarsely ground black pepper. Serve piled up on tender young spinach leaves, scatter with torn basil and more coarsely ground black pepper.

Omelet "tagliatelle" salad

serves 2

calorie count 500kcal; fat
    content 23g per serving

4 eggs

2 tablespoons chopped
    fresh parsley

salt and freshly ground
    black pepper

olive oil for frying

for the salad

2 red bell peppers,
    halved and deseeded

1 oakleaf lettuce, washed
    and torn into pieces

2 large tomatoes,
    skinned and sliced

10–12 black olives

small bunch of fresh
    chives, snipped

12 fresh basil leaves, torn

for the dressing

½ teaspoon Dijon mustard

1 garlic clove, crushed

1 tablespoon red wine
    vinegar

4 tablespoons olive oil

A salad originally created by Prue Leith inspired this recipe—which I have adapted quite a bit—with its ribbons of omelet.

A very nutritious main-course salad, with the eggs, lettuce, and olives providing iron plus loads of vitamin C to make the most of it.

To make the omelet "tagliatelle", whisk the eggs in a bowl with the chopped parsley and season with salt and pepper. Heat 1–2 teaspoons of olive oil in a small skillet, tip in half the egg mixture, and cook over gentle heat, pushing the egg into the middle of the skillet as it cooks, until set. Invert the cooked omelet on to a plate and make another with the remaining egg, using more oil if necessary. When cool, roll up the omelets loosely and cut them into thin strips. Set aside.

For the salad, place the pepper halves under a preheated broiler, shiny side up, and cook for 10–15 minutes, or until they are charred and blistered in places. Remove from the broiler, cover with a plate until cool enough to handle, then cut the peppers into thick strips.

Meanwhile, make the dressing by placing all the ingredients and a seasoning of salt and pepper in a small screw-top jar and shaking well to combine the ingredients.

Place the torn lettuce leaves in a bowl. Add 1–2 tablespoons of the dressing and toss the lettuce, using a spoon or your hands, until lightly coated.

Divide the lettuce between two plates. Arrange the strips of omelet and red pepper, the tomatoes and olives on top. Scatter the chives and basil over the salad, drizzle the remaining dressing on top, and serve at once.

quick fixes for the end of the day

Fast vegetables

The first group of recipes in this section comprise vegetable-based main courses that can be cooked on top of the stove. These are often enhanced by some kind of starchy accompaniment, and there are many to choose from—warm, good bread, for example. Think of Indian naan bread, Italian focaccia, country rye, or multi-grain bread, Middle Eastern sesame bread, and so on. Multiply this with flavorings like sun-dried tomato, cumin, onion, cheese, or walnuts, and you realize the scope. One or two interesting breads or some rolls in the freezer, for quick reheating, will be useful for times when you just can't get to a store.

Other complex carbohydrates that I find particularly useful to keep in stock for serving with these vegetable main courses are couscous and rice. With the easy-to-use brands now available, couscous couldn't be simpler—just follow the package instructions. These probably tell you to soak the couscous in boiling water in a saucepan for a few minutes, perhaps with a little olive oil or butter added—although this can be omitted—then heat gently.

There are several ways of cooking rice, but the quickest is what I call the pasta method. Simply add the rice to a saucepan containing plenty of boiling water, just as you would pasta. Give it a stir, then cook until tender. This takes about 8 minutes for white basmati rice, 12 minutes for long-grain white rice, 15–20 minutes for brown basmati, and about 40 minutes for long-grain brown rice—but check individual labels for details. When the rice is cooked, drain into a large strainer, rinse with boiling water from a kettle, put back into the saucepan, and keep it warm until you are ready to serve it.

Thick spinach omelet

serves 2

calorie count 280kcal; fat
content 21g per serving

8 ounces spinach

salt and freshly ground
black pepper

1 tablespoon olive oil

4 eggs, beaten

½ ounce Parmesan
cheese, grated

Serve this omelet with a tomato and black olive salad and some hot bread. It is also nice eaten cold, with salad.

Packed with iron, protein, vitamin C, potassium, riboflavin, thiamin, and zinc, it also provides one and a half times the recommended daily allowance for folic acid and beta-carotene.

Wash the spinach and place it in a large saucepan with just the water clinging to the leaves. Cook for 5–6 minutes, until wilted and tender, then drain in a colander. Chop the spinach roughly and season with salt and pepper.

Heat the oil in a skillet and add the spinach, then pour in the beaten eggs. Cook gently, continually pushing the egg into the middle of the skillet as it cooks, until the base is set. Sprinkle the Parmesan cheese over the top, then place the skillet under a preheated broiler for 4–5 minutes, to cook and set the top of the omelet. Serve cut into thick wedges.

Purple-sprouting broccoli with golden pepper cannellini cream

serves 2

calorie count 160kcal; fat content 0.5g per serving

1 large yellow bell pepper, deseeded and roughly chopped

1 garlic clove, sliced or chopped

14-ounce can cannellini beans, drained

juice of ½ lemon

salt and freshly ground black pepper

10 ounces purple-sprouting broccoli, trimmed

Cooked yellow bell peppers, puréed with cannellini beans, make this creamy, slightly sweet-tasting sauce/dip, which goes well with broiled vegetables, on bread, or served with purple-sprouting broccoli, as here.

Broccoli is possibly the most nutritious vegetable, rich in calcium, beta-carotene, vitamins C and B6, iron, potassium, riboflavin, and masses of folic acid.

Place the yellow pepper in a small saucepan, add enough water to give a depth of about ½ inch. Bring to a boil, cover, and cook gently for 10–15 minutes, until the pepper is very tender. Drain, then place the chunks of pepper and garlic in a blender or food processor with the drained cannellini beans, lemon juice, and a little salt and pepper. Whiz to a smooth purée; taste, and add more salt and pepper as required. Adjust the consistency of the purée to suit your taste by adding a little water.

Cook the broccoli in a saucepan containing a little rapidly boiling water for about 7 minutes, or until tender. Drain and serve at once with the pepper and cannellini bean cream.

Mushrooms and chestnuts
with parsley mashed potatoes

serves 2

calorie count 530kcal; fat
content 14g per serving

for the gravy

2 teaspoons olive oil

1 onion, finely chopped

6 ounces chestnut
mushrooms, sliced

2 garlic cloves, chopped

1 tablespoon all-purpose
flour

2 tablespoons Madeira

1 vegetable or mushroom
stock cube, dissolved in
1¼ cups water

1 tablespoon soy sauce

6 ounces cooked chestnuts

salt and freshly ground
black pepper

for the potatoes

1½ pounds potatoes,
peeled and cut into
½-inch pieces

1 tablespoon olive oil

1 tablespoon chopped
fresh parsley

salt and freshly ground
black pepper

This is wonderfully comforting: mushrooms and chestnuts in rich gravy with creamy potatoes. Canned or vacuum-packed chestnuts, which are already cooked and skinned, are quite widely available.

This size serving of chestnuts (3 ounces per person) contains less than 2g of fat yet provides useful amounts of folic acid, potassium, vitamin B6, and thiamin.

Start by making the gravy. Heat the oil in a large saucepan, add the onion and fry for 5 minutes, until beginning to soften and brown. Add the mushrooms and garlic and cook for a further 2–3 minutes. Sprinkle in the flour and stir over the heat, letting it brown a little. Add the Madeira and let it bubble up, then pour in the stock, stirring until thickened. Add the soy sauce and chestnuts, then let it simmer gently, uncovered, while you cook the potatoes.

Cook the potatoes in a large saucepan of water for about 20 minutes, or until tender. Drain them, reserving the water. Mash the potatoes with the olive oil and enough of the cooking water to give a creamy consistency. Add the chopped parsley, and salt and pepper to taste.

Taste the gravy and season with salt and pepper if required, then serve with the mashed potatoes.

Spiced cauliflower and peas

serves 2–3

calorie count 250–330 kcal; fat content 5–8g per serving

1 tablespoon olive oil

1 onion, finely chopped

1 teaspoon cumin seeds

2 garlic cloves, crushed

¼ teaspoon turmeric

1 pound tomatoes, skinned and chopped, or 14-ounce can chopped tomatoes

salt and freshly ground black pepper

1 medium cauliflower, trimmed and divided into smallish flowerets

scant 1 cup frozen petits pois (small peas)

small bunch of fresh cilantro, chopped

Cauliflower is quick to prepare—even more so if you buy ready-prepared flowerets. Serve this dish with some warm naan bread or rice, with sweet mango chutney and, for a creamy touch, yogurt mixed with chopped chives or cilantro.

Plentiful in vitamin C to pep you up, as well as folic acid from the cauliflower and the antioxidant lycopene—from the tomatoes—for a healthy heart.

Heat the oil in a large saucepan and add the onion. Cover and cook gently for 7 minutes, until tender but not browned. Add the cumin seeds and garlic and fry for 30 seconds, then stir in the turmeric and cook for another few seconds. Add the tomatoes and cook, uncovered, for about 15 minutes, until the liquid has evaporated.

Season with salt and pepper, add the cauliflower flowerets and stir to coat them with the tomato mixture. If the peas are very icy, place them in a strainer and pour boiling wate over them, then add them to the mixture. Cook for 4–5 minutes, or until the cauliflower is just tender. Check the seasoning, add the cilantro, and serve.

Variation: Spiced green beans

Use 8 ounces slim green beans, lightly trimmed as necessary, instead of cauliflower and peas. This makes a smaller amount—enough to serve 2 people.

Quick Bombay potatoes

serves 2

calorie count 280kcal; fat content 8g per serving

1 pound potatoes, peeled and cut into ½-inch pieces

1 onion, chopped

1 tablespoon olive oil

1 garlic clove, crushed

2 teaspoons each ground cumin and ground coriander, or 2–3 teaspoons curry powder to taste

salt and freshly ground black pepper

A few basic storecupboard ingredients are all you need to make this speedy, filling dish, for which you do need some curry powder or paste, or preferably some curry spices. If you happen to have a cilantro plant on the kitchen windowsill or a bunch of cilantro tucked away in the fridge, some of this snipped over the top makes it extra good. Serve with warm naan bread or basmati rice; some mango chutney as an accompaniment never goes amiss and I like sliced tomatoes with it, too.

Place the potatoes in a saucepan and pour in enough water just to cover. Cook for about 15 minutes, or until tender but not breaking up at all. Drain, reserving the liquid.

Meanwhile, fry the onion in the oil for 7 minutes or so, until almost tender, then add the garlic and spices and cook for 1–2 minutes more. Add the cooked potatoes and stir gently but thoroughly, adding 1–2 tablespoons of the reserved cooking water if necessary, to loosen the mixture. Cook gently for 3–4 minutes to heat through and blend the flavors. Season with salt and pepper and serve.

Variation: Quick Bombay potatoes with green peas

Frozen peas, preferably petits pois, make an attractive and nutritious addition, as they contain plenty of vitamin C. Place 1⅔ cups frozen peas in a strainer and pour boiling water over them. Add to the potato mixture and heat through.

Variation: Quick Bombay potatoes with garbanzos

For another tasty variation, packed with protein, drain a 14-ounce can of garbanzos (chickpeas) and add to the spicy onion with the potatoes.

Spicy eggplant and garbanzos

serves 3

calorie count 290kcal; fat content 6g per serving

1 tablespoon olive oil

1½ teaspoons cumin seeds

1 dried red chili pepper

1 garlic clove, crushed

12 ounces potatoes, peeled and cut into ½-inch dice

12 ounces eggplant, cut into ½-inch dice

12 ounces white mushrooms, halved

¼ teaspoon turmeric

1 teaspoon ground coriander

1¼ cups passata (strained tomatoes)

2¼ teaspoons salt

3 ounces chopped fresh cilantro leaves (and root, if attached)

14-ounce can garbanzos (chickpeas)

1¾ cups water or vegetable stock

This is my slightly adapted version of one of Madhur Jaffrey's recipes. It's not one you can make absolutely in a flash, but the preparation is easy and once all the ingredients are in the pan you can sit back and relax while it cooks. Serve with some warm Indian bread, such as garlic naan, and a bowl of thick creamy yogurt if you wish.

Rich in protein, iron, folic acid, and zinc; low in fat, easy to make, and satisfying to eat—what more could one ask for?

Heat the oil in a large saucepan. Add the cumin seeds and cook for a few seconds until they start to sizzle and pop. Crumble in the chili pepper and add the garlic, potatoes, eggplant, mushrooms, turmeric, and ground coriander. Stir over the heat for a few seconds to coat all the vegetables with the spices, then pour in the passata and add the salt, cilantro, garbanzos and their liquid, and water or stock.

Bring to a boil, then cover and cook gently for about 30 minutes, until the vegetables are tender. Check the seasoning, then serve.

Potato, spinach, and garbanzos with cumin

serves 2–3

calorie count 290–450 kcal; fat content 5–8g per serving

1 small onion, finely chopped

2 teaspoons olive oil

1 teaspoon cumin seeds

¼ teaspoon turmeric

2 garlic cloves, crushed

1 pound potatoes, peeled and cut into ¼-inch dice

8 ounces tender spinach leaves, washed

1 dried red chili pepper, crumbled

salt

14-ounce can garbanzos, drained and rinsed

Serve with warm naan bread, plain yogurt with some chopped fresh cilantro stirred into it, sliced firm tomatoes, and mango chutney.

Very rich in complex carbohydrates, this is a sustaining dish. It's also a good source of iron and vitamin C, potassium, calcium, and B vitamins.

Fry the onion in the oil for 4–5 minutes, until it is beginning to soften, then add the cumin seeds, turmeric, and garlic, and fry for a further 2–3 minutes. Add the potatoes, spinach, crumbled chili, and a little salt to taste. Stir well, then cover and cook gently for 7–8 minutes, until the potatoes are tender. The spinach will produce some liquid, but keep an eye on it and stir often to prevent sticking.

Finally, add the drained garbanzos, and cook gently until heated through. Check the seasoning and serve.

Garbanzo curry

serves 2

calorie count 250kcal; fat
content 15g per serving

12 ounces prepared
cauliflower and
broccoli flowerets

2 tomatoes, chopped

14-ounce can garbanzos
(chickpeas), drained

2 tablespoons balti
curry paste

salt

chopped fresh cilantro,
to garnish

Simply cook a package of ready-prepared broccoli and cauliflower, mix with a can of garbanzos, some fresh tomato, and some curry paste and you have a very tasty curry that only needs some Indian bread or quickly cooked basmati rice (see page 64) to make a satisfying meal. You can buy curry paste at specialty food stores—balti curry paste is my favorite, although there are other types worth trying.

Very health-giving as well as delicious, this dish is packed with vitamins and minerals as well as protein and high-energy carbohydrates.

Pour water into a medium-large saucepan to a depth of ½ inch and bring to a boil. Add the prepared vegetables and cook for 4–5 minutes, until just tender. Drain, then return to the warm pan.

Add the tomatoes, garbanzos, and curry paste, and cook gently for 3–4 minutes until the mixture is hot. Stir often to prevent the mixture from sticking to the pan—if it looks a bit dry, add 1–2 tablespoons of water. Season to taste, then serve sprinkled with chopped cilantro.

Lentil dhal

serves 4

calorie count 280kcal;
  fat content less than
  1g per serving

1 cup split red lentils

1 onion, sliced

a walnut-sized piece
  of fresh gingerroot,
  peeled and sliced

1 green chili pepper

½ teaspoon turmeric

1 bay leaf

4 cups water

2 teaspoons ground cumin

2 teaspoons ground
  coriander

2 tablespoons lemon juice

salt

2 tablespoons chopped
  fresh cilantro, to garnish
  (optional)

Dhal is quick and easy to make. It is low in fat, turns a plate of cooked vegetables or rice into a protein-rich meal, and can be gently spiced or fiery hot according to taste. This quantity of dhal is enough for four people—I don't think it is worth making a smaller quantity since the dhal goes on improving as the flavors blend. So, if there is some left over, it is even better the next day. Serve with warm Indian bread, a salad of sliced tomatoes and onions, and mango chutney. It is also the perfect accompaniment to cooked purple-sprouting broccoli.

A wonderful source of iron—a cup of cooked lentils provides two-thirds of the recommended daily allowance of iron—as well as B vitamins, zinc, protein, and complex carbohydrates.

Place the lentils in a saucepan with the onion, fresh gingerroot, whole chili, turmeric, bay leaf, and water. Bring to a boil, then reduce the heat and let simmer for 20–25 minutes, until the lentils are very soft and pale-colored. Add a little more water if the mixture looks very thick—the consistency is up to you—then stir in the cumin, ground coriander, lemon juice, and salt to taste.

Garnish with chopped cilantro, if using, just before serving.

Variation: Spinach dhal
Spinach dhal is a very pleasant variation. Add ½ pound tender young spinach leaves to the dhal with the ground cumin and coriander, lemon juice, and salt, and cook for 10 minutes more, until the spinach is tender and wilted. Serve at once.

Thai vegetable stir-fry

serves 2

calorie count 470kcal; fat
content 22g per serving

²⁄₃ cup rice

2 teaspoons toasted
sesame oil

1 onion, chopped

1 small red bell pepper,
deseeded and
thinly sliced

1–2 tablespoons Thai
red curry paste

scant 1 cup unsweetened
coconut milk

²⁄₃ cup water

4 ounces baby corn,
halved lengthways

4 ounces snow peas,
halved lengthways

4 ounces zucchini,
cut into ¼-inch slices

salt

2 tablespoons chopped
fresh cilantro

This is an easy supper using shop-bought Thai curry paste—read the label before you buy it to make sure it doesn't contain fish (see page 140). Serve with white basmati rice, or fragrant Thai jasmine rice for a real treat.

Get the rice on to cook before you start making the stir-fry. Bring a large saucepan of water to a boil, add the rice, and cook according to package instructions until tender. Drain when cooked.

To make the stir-fry, heat the sesame oil in a large saucepan or wok and add the onion and red pepper. Cook for 5 minutes, until beginning to soften, then stir in the Thai curry paste, coconut milk, and water. Bring to a boil, then add the corn, snow peas, zucchini, and a little salt to taste. Cook gently for about 5 minutes, until the vegetables are tender. Check the seasoning, then add the cilantro, and serve with the rice.

Sweet and sour bean curd stir-fry

serves 2

calorie count 300kcal; fat content 17g per serving

4 teaspoons toasted sesame oil

8–10-ounce package of firm bean curd, drained and cut into thin pieces

1 carrot, cut into matchsticks

1 zucchini, cut into matchsticks

4 ounces snow peas, halved

8 scallions, sliced

8-ounce can water chestnuts, drained and halved

for the sauce

½ teaspoon cornstarch

2 tablespoons tamari or other soy sauce

1 teaspoon sugar

1 tablespoon clear honey

1 tablespoon sherry

1 tablespoon rice vinegar

This is quick to make as it is, but you could speed it up even more if you use a package of ready-prepared stir-fry vegetables instead of the ones specified here, although they take only minutes to prepare.

Bean curd has been shown to have powerful anti-carcinogenic properties, and is also a rich source of phytoestrogens (see page 8).

Heat 2 teaspoons of the sesame oil in a skillet or wok, add the pieces of bean curd and fry on both sides until crisp and golden brown. This will take about 4–5 minutes on each side, and you may need to do it in two batches, depending on the size of your pan, so get this started before you begin work on the vegetables.

While the bean curd is cooking, mix together the sauce ingredients in a small bowl and set aside.

Heat the remaining sesame oil in a wok and add all the vegetables. Stir-fry for 3–4 minutes, until heated through but still crunchy. Give the sauce a quick stir, then pour it into the wok and stir until it has thickened. Add the bean curd, stir until coated with the sauce, then serve with rice or noodles.

Broccoli and smoky bean curd in hoisin sauce

serves 2

calorie count 330kcal; fat content 17g per serving

1 pound broccoli flowerets

1 tablespoon toasted sesame oil

8–10-ounce package of smoked bean curd, drained and cut into thin pieces

4 tablespoons hoisin sauce

1 tablespoon soy sauce

salt and freshly ground black pepper

This is one of my favorite ways of cooking broccoli, combined with crisp little pieces of smoky bean curd in a sweet sauce. Serve with plain rice. Short-grain brown rice is good with this but takes 45 minutes to cook; for greater speed and an equally delicious result, use white rice and don't "fluff" it—it's nice with the grains sticking together, Asian-style, and ideal for eating with chopsticks.

Packed with nutrients but particularly rich in calcium and phytoestrogens for healthy bones and well-balanced hormones.

Cook the broccoli in a saucepan of boiling water until just tender— about 4 minutes. Drain and return to the warm saucepan.

Meanwhile, heat the sesame oil in a skillet or wok and fry the bean curd on both sides, until crisp and golden brown.

Add the bean curd to the broccoli, together with the hoisin and soy sauces, and salt and pepper to taste. Cook gently for 3–4 minutes, stirring, until heated through, then serve with rice.

Japanese cabbage and ginger pancake

serves 2

calorie count 320kcal;
   fat content 22g per
   serving (without the
   mayonnaise and HP
   Sauce topping)

1 cup all-purpose flour
2 good pinches of sugar
salt
about ⅔ cup cold water
1 egg
1 ounce pickled ginger,
   shredded
5 ounces white cabbage,
   finely shredded
1 carrot, grated
vegetable oil for frying

to serve
HP Sauce
mayonnaise
powdered seaweed

A friend and I had this dish for lunch at the Yaohan Plaza Japanese shopping center in north London, now no longer there. We sat at a shiny, clean, heated counter, and watched as our cook/waitress mixed the ingredients together then cooked it on the counter in front of us. There is a recipe for something similar in Japanese Vegetarian Cookery by Patricia Richfield, and this is my slightly adapted version. Serve it on its own or with Ginger miso broth (see page 33).

Research has shown that people who regularly eat cruciferous vegetables, such as cabbage, have a lower risk of contracting certain cancers. As little as one weekly serving of cabbage may be enough to reduce the risk of cancer of the colon by half.

Sift the flour into a bowl, add the sugar and a little salt, then mix in the water, egg, pickled ginger, cabbage, and carrot. Heat about 1 tablespoon of oil in a skillet. Pour in the batter mixture and spread out to a circle. Reduce the heat to low and cover the skillet.

Fry for about 10 minutes until the base is golden brown. Then turn the pancake over and fry, uncovered, for a further 5–6 minutes. While cooking, cut the top in a few places with a knife to let the steam escape.

To serve, invert on to a warmed plate, spread about 2–3 tablespoons HP Sauce over the top, then a similar amount of mayonnaise, and sprinkle with powdered seaweed. Cut in half and serve.

Japanese vegetables on sushi rice

serves 2

calorie count 400kcal;
fat content less than
1g per serving

1 cup Japanese round-
grain rice (see right)
1 cup water
3 tablespoons rice vinegar
4 teaspoons sugar
1 teaspoon salt

for the vegetables
1 carrot, cut into
matchsticks
4 ounces slim green
beans, trimmed as
necessary and cut
into 2-inch lengths
4 ounces snow peas
8 scallions, sliced
2 tablespoons tamari
or other soy sauce
1 teaspoon sugar
1 sheet of toasted nori
(see page 138)
2 teaspoons Gomasio
(see page 37)
or toasted sesame
seeds for sprinkling

Easy, filling, and low in fat… This is best made with Japanese rice, which clumps together as it cooks; however, I have also made it with risotto rice, with round-grain brown rice—the healthiest option but takes 40–45 minutes to cook—and even, when really pressed, ordinary long-grain white rice, mashed a bit to make it stickier.

A delicious and unusual way of serving vegetables, this includes health-giving sesame seeds and nori, which is made from laver seaweed and is a concentrated source of many nutrients, including iron, carotene, niacin, and even protein.

Wash the rice in a strainer under cold water until the water runs clear, then leave the rice to drain (and swell) in the strainer for 20 minutes.

Put the rice in a saucepan with the water. Boil for 10 minutes, stir, then boil for a further 5 minutes. Remove from the heat, cover, and leave for 15 minutes. Stir in the vinegar, sugar, and salt.

Next, cook the vegetables. Add the carrot and beans to a saucepan of boiling water. Cover and cook for 4–5 minutes, or until the vegetables are almost tender, then add the snow peas and scallions, and cook for 2 minutes longer. Drain, then mix with the soy sauce and sugar.

Divide the sticky rice between two warm plates. Spoon the vegetables on top, then crumble or snip over the toasted nori and scatter with a little Gomasio or toasted sesame seeds.

Pasta, noodles, rice, and polenta

The recipes in this section use starchy foods, or complex carbohydrates, as their main ingredient.

Pasta really doesn't need any introduction; it is probably what first springs to mind when we think of quick cooking. If you like pasta, do experiment with noodles, which are even quicker to cook and great with Asian flavorings, such as toasted sesame oil and seeds, grated fresh gingerroot, soy sauce, garlic, and the odd splash of sherry, sake, or mirin, if you are in the mood.

Now that quick-cooking or "instant" polenta is widely available, this is another ingredient that can form the basis of a meal with a good, tasty sauce or some roasted vegetables to accompany it. One of my favorite ways of eating polenta is with a ragout of mushrooms, including some wild ones, although its mashed-potato-like quality means that it goes well with many other vegetable mixtures.

Asian noodle and vegetable stir-fry

serves 2

calorie count 220kcal; fat
   content 7g per serving

3 ounces thin egg noodles
2 teaspoons toasted
   sesame oil
1 garlic clove, crushed
½-inch piece of fresh
   gingerroot, grated
2 zucchini, very thinly
   cut on the diagonal
8 ounces broccoli
   flowerets, very
   thinly sliced
1 tablespoon soy sauce

A light-but-filling, quick, delicious mixture of noodles and vegetables with Asian flavorings.

This an excellent way of serving broccoli, which a panel of US nutritionists voted as the top vegetable for nutrients.

Add the noodles to a large saucepan of boiling water and simmer for 3–4 minutes, or according to package instructions, until al dente. Drain well.

When the noodles are almost cooked, heat the sesame oil in a large saucepan or wok. Add the garlic and gingerroot and stir-fry for a few seconds. Add the zucchini and broccoli and stir-fry for 1–2 minutes, until heated through but still crunchy. Add the noodles and the soy sauce, toss everything together, and serve at once.

Rice noodle stir-fry with peanut sauce

serves 2

calorie count 400kcal; fat
content 7g per serving

4 ounces Chinese rice
noodles
2 teaspoons toasted
sesame oil
6 scallions, sliced
4 ounces baby corn, halved
4 ounces snow peas,
halved
4 ounces Asian greens
such as bok choy or
napa cabbage, shredded

for the stir-fry sauce
1 tablespoon crunchy
peanut butter
1 tablespoon soy sauce
1 tablespoon sherry
1 tablespoon rice vinegar
1 garlic clove, crushed
½ teaspoon light brown
sugar

I love these noodles because all the cooking they need is a soak in boiling water. Get them soaking while you deal with the vegetables, mix them all together, et voilà—you have your meal.

Peanuts are rich in protein, minerals, and vitamins, particularly niacin. Here, they make a tasty Thai-style peanut sauce to go with a mixture of fresh vegetables.

Place the rice noodles in a large bowl, cover with boiling water and leave for 4 minutes, or according to package instructions.

Meanwhile, make the stir-fry sauce by mixing together all the ingredients in a small bowl. Set aside.

Heat the sesame oil in a large saucepan or wok, add the prepared vegetables, and stir-fry for 2 minutes. Meanwhile, drain the noodles in a colander, then add them to the vegetables, together with the stir-fry sauce. Stir-fry for about 2 minutes, until everything is mixed and heated through—you have to stir quite firmly to integrate the tangle of noodles with the sauce and vegetables. Serve at once.

Japanese-style shiitake mushrooms on sticky rice with nori and sesame

serves 2

calorie count 250kcal; fat content 5g per serving

⅔ cup Japanese round-grain rice (see right)

1¼ cups water

8 ounces fresh shiitake mushrooms

1 tablespoon toasted sesame oil

4 tablespoons mirin

4 tablespoons sake

4 tablespoons tamari or other soy sauce

2 x 4-inch squares of nori seaweed (see page 138)

2 teaspoons Gomasio (see page 37) or toasted sesame seeds

3–4 lengths of fresh chives

Japanese glutinous rice is ideal for this recipe; otherwise use a risotto rice, round-grain dessert rice or round-grain organic brown rice. The idea is that the grains of rice stick together so that you can eat it in clumps. The rice is piled on to squares of black nori seaweed and topped with the mushrooms, bathed in their syrupy juices, and a scattering of toasted sesame seeds.

Nori is so nutritious that everyone could benefit from eating a sheet of it every day, but can be omitted if you can't get it. Shiitake mushrooms are revered in the East for their health-giving and medicinal properties.

Place the rice in a heavy-bottomed saucepan with the water. Bring to a boil, then turn the heat down very low—perhaps put the pan on a heat diffuser if you have one. (I never add salt to rice when it is being served as an accompaniment like this.) Let the rice cook gently until the grains are tender and all the water has been absorbed— about 20 minutes for white rice, double that for brown.

Meanwhile, wipe the mushrooms and trim the stems slightly as necessary. Slice or halve the mushrooms, or leave them whole if preferred. Heat the oil in a saucepan and add the mushrooms. Cook them over moderately high heat for 5 minutes, until tender, then add the mirin, sake, and tamari. Let the mixture bubble over the heat for 1–2 minutes until it has reduced to a thick, glossy syrup

If using untoasted nori, take one square at a time and, using tongs, hold it over a stove-top burner, about 4 inches from the heat, for a few seconds until crisp, then cook the other side.

Place a square of nori in the center of each plate and pile the rice on top. Spoon the mushrooms over the rice, then scatter with the Gomasio or toasted sesame seeds, and some long pieces of chive.

Crisp noodle cakes with shiitake mushrooms, bok choy, and chili pepper

serves 2

calorie count 490kcal; fat
content 25g per serving

4 ounces thin egg noodles

I tablespoon shoyu or
tamari soy sauce

salt

I–2 tablespoons toasted
sesame oil

for the vegetables

4 ounces fresh shiitake
mushrooms

10 ounces bok choy
(pak choi)

4 teaspoons toasted
sesame oil

I garlic clove, finely sliced

I teaspoon cornstarch

2 tablespoons teriyaki
sauce, or shoyu, or
tamari soy sauce

salt

I½ teaspoons red chili
pepper sauce or paste

½ teaspoon water

This is modeled on a glorious lunch that my daughter Kate and I enjoyed at Roscoff's (now renamed Cayenne) in Belfast, Ireland. Crisp noodles are topped with stir-fried vegetables and flecked with drops of scarlet chili pepper sauce.

Shiitake mushrooms and bok choy both have health-giving properties.

Put the noodles into a saucepan of rapidly boiling water and cook for about 3 minutes, or according to the package instructions, until al dente. Drain well and add the soy sauce and a little salt to taste.

Heat 1 tablespoon of sesame oil in a large skillet, preferably non-stick. Add half the noodles, forming them into a flat, oval cake, slightly less than ½ inch thick. Push to one side of the skillet to make room for another similar cake. Cook over moderate heat for 4–5 minutes, until the undersides are a deep golden brown, then turn them with a fish slice and cook the other side, adding a little more oil if necessary. They will take a good 4 minutes to get really crisp.

Meanwhile, stir-fry the vegetables. Wipe the mushrooms and trim the stems slightly as necessary, then slice. Wash the bok choy, trim if necessary, then slice. Heat 3 teaspoons of the oil in a large sauce-pan or wok and add the garlic. Cook for 30 seconds, then add the mushrooms. Stir-fry over moderately high heat for 3 minutes, until beginning to soften, then add the bok choy and stir-fry for a further 3–4 minutes, until it is wilted and tender but still crisp. Mix the cornstarch with the teriyaki or soy sauce and add to the pan; cook for 1–2 minutes to thicken. Taste and add a little salt if necessary.

Mix the chili pepper sauce or paste with the water. Arrange a noodle cake and half the vegetables on each plate; put drops of the chili-water mixture around the edge, then serve immediately.

Porcini risotto

serves 4

calorie count 370kcal; fat content 7g per serving

1/3 ounce dried porcini mushrooms

1 mushroom stock cube

2 cups boiling water

1 teaspoon olive oil

1 ounce butter

1 onion, finely chopped

1 garlic clove, chopped

2 cups arborio or carnaroli rice

1 glass of white wine, vermouth, or sherry

1 tablespoon freshly grated Parmesan cheese, plus extra to serve

salt and freshly ground black pepper

One of my favorite "storecupboard" dishes, this is easy to make and one of the most satisfying and comforting quick dishes I know. It's the dried porcini mushrooms with their deep, smoky flavor, together with the creamy risotto rice, that make this. Having said that, I have made it with ordinary long-grain rice and a splash of leftover red wine along with the porcini, and it was still wonderful. Serve just as it is, or with some lightly dressed salad leaves or tomato salad on the side.

Rice is rich in carbohydrates but also contains some protein; it is gluten-free and helps to stabilize blood sugar levels.

Place the porcini in a measuring pitcher, crumble in the stock cube, and add the boiling water. Set aside.

Heat the oil and half the butter in a large, heavy-bottomed saucepan over medium heat. Add the onion and garlic and fry gently for 5 minutes, until beginning to soften, then add the rice and stir until the grains are coated with the buttery juices.

Pour in the wine, vermouth, or sherry. Let the mixture bubble away, then stir in 2 tablespoons of the mushroom stock—without removing the porcini from the pitcher—stirring over moderate heat until the liquid has been absorbed. Then add another 2 tablespoons of stock and continue in this way until the rice is cooked—about 20 minutes. Chop the soaked porcini and add them to the rice with the last of the stock. If you have added all the stock and the rice is not quite done, or it is a bit dry, just add a little more hot water. Then beat in the remaining butter and the Parmesan cheese. Check the seasoning and serve with a grinding of black pepper and extra Parmesan on top.

Fettuccine with walnuts, garlic, and butter

serves 2

calorie count 540kcal; fat
content 15g per serving

7 ounces dried fettuccine

¼ cup shelled walnuts

½ ounce butter
or 1 tablespoon olive
or walnut oil

1 garlic clove, crushed

salt and freshly ground
black pepper

Simple but very good. If you have freshly cracked walnuts, so much the better.

Walnuts are rich in thiamin, vitamin B6, folic acid, iron, and zinc.

Plunge the pasta into a saucepan of rapidly boiling, salted water and cook according to package instructions, until al dente.

Meanwhile, spread the walnuts on a baking sheet and place under a hot broiler for 1–2 minutes until lightly browned. Remove from the broiler, let cool slightly, then grind finely using a food processor, a pestle and mortar, or a small rotary hand grater. Take care not to over-process the walnuts, which would make them oily.

Drain the cooked pasta and return it to the still-warm saucepan with the butter or oil, garlic, and ground walnuts. Toss the pasta gently until coated with the walnuts, then spoon into warmed serving bowls, grind over some pepper, and serve at once.

Tagliatelle with spinach, goat cheese, and capers

serves 2

calorie count 650kcal; fat
    content 24g per serving

7 ounces dried tagliatelle

2 tablespoons olive oil

2 garlic cloves, finely sliced

4 ounces tender young
    spinach leaves, washed

3 ounces firm goat
    cheese, crumbled

1 tablespoon capers
    or caper berries

salt and freshly ground
    black pepper

Spinach and pasta is a classic combination, enlivened here by the sharpness of goat cheese and capers.

This recipe provides complex carbohydrates from the pasta, together with carotene, vitamin C, folic acid, and potassium from the spinach.

Plunge the pasta into a saucepan of rapidly boiling, salted water and cook according to package instructions, until al dente.

Just before the pasta is ready, heat 1 tablespoon of the oil in a saucepan over medium heat, add the garlic, and cook for 1–2 minutes until just beginning to color. Remove from the heat, add the spinach, and toss for a few seconds until it has wilted.

Drain the cooked pasta and return it to the still-warm saucepan with the remaining oil. Mix well, then tip the pasta into warmed serving bowls. Top with the spinach and garlic mixture, the crumbled goat cheese, capers or caper berries, and a grinding of black pepper, and serve at once.

Penne with sun-dried tomato paste, basil, and olives

serves 2

calorie count 650kcal; fat content 26g per serving

7 ounces dried penne

2 tablespoons sun-dried tomato paste

I garlic clove, crushed

2 ounces small black olives, such as Niçoise

6 good-sized sprigs of fresh basil, torn

salt and freshly ground black pepper

I ounce fresh Parmesan cheese, cut into flakes

Here I have used sun-dried tomato paste rather like pesto, to coat the pasta deliciously.

A wonderfully satisfying and tasty dish, high in complex carbohydrates.

Plunge the pasta into a saucepan of rapidly boiling, salted water and cook according to package instructions, until al dente.

Drain the pasta and return it to the still-warm saucepan, together with the sun-dried tomato paste and garlic. Toss the pasta gently to coat it with the tomato paste and garlic, then add the olives and torn basil. Spoon the pasta into warmed serving bowls and grind over some pepper. Top with the Parmesan and serve at once.

Fusilli with oyster mushrooms and artichokes

serves 2

calorie count 590kcal; fat
   content 8g per serving
   (without Parmesan)

7 ounces dried fusilli,
   conchiglie, penne,
   or other short,
   chunky pasta
1 tablespoon olive oil
1 garlic clove, crushed
4 ounces oyster
   mushrooms, torn into
   bite-sized pieces if large
14-ounce can artichoke
   hearts, drained and
   sliced, or 14 ounces
   frozen artichoke
   bottoms, thawed
salt and freshly ground
   black pepper
6 good sprigs of basil, torn
1 ounce fresh Parmesan
   cheese, cut into flakes
   (optional)

I'm particularly fond of both oyster mushrooms and artichokes and I love putting them together with pasta. I use canned artichokes rather than a jar of artichoke hearts in oil because it cuts down the fat content of the dish. Alternatively, if you live near a store that stocks Middle Eastern foods, look for frozen artichoke bottoms, which are delectable and can be used instead.

Artichokes contain cynarin, which is believed to have significant liver-protecting and regenerating effects; they may also help to control cholesterol levels.

Plunge the pasta into a saucepan of rapidly boiling, salted water and cook according to package instructions, until al dente.

Meanwhile, heat the oil in a skillet and fry the garlic for a few seconds, then add the mushrooms and cook until tender—about 5 minutes. Add the artichokes, season with salt and pepper, and keep warm until the pasta is ready.

Drain the cooked pasta and return it to the still-warm saucepan, together with the mushroom and artichoke mixture and the basil. Toss the pasta gently, then serve at once, handing the Parmesan separately at the table.

Fusilli with tomato sauce and garbanzos

serves 2

calorie count 420kcal; fat content 8g per serving

1 tablespoon olive oil

1 onion, finely chopped

1 garlic clove, crushed

14-ounce can tomatoes in juice

½ x 14-ounce can garbanzos (chickpeas), drained

salt and freshly ground black pepper

7 ounces dried fusilli

This recipe is an old friend, and a useful one to know. I love it with garbanzos, but you could use other types of canned beans to give body and flavor—cannellini or borlotti beans, for instance.

A dish that's packed with protein, thanks to the combination of the wheat-plus-pulse provided by the pasta and garbanzos; plus valuable minerals and B vitamins.

Start making the sauce while you heat up a large saucepan of water for the pasta. Heat the oil in a saucepan, add the onion and garlic, and cook gently for about 7 minutes, until softened but not browned. Add the tomatoes and their juice, breaking them up with a spoon, then cook uncovered for about 15 minutes, until thick. Add the drained garbanzos and season with salt and pepper.

Meanwhile, cook the pasta in the saucepan of rapidly boiling, salted water according to package instructions, until al dente. Drain the pasta and spoon into two warmed serving bowls. Pour the sauce on top, grind over some pepper, and serve at once.

Rigatoni with broiled eggplant, feta cheese, and cherry tomatoes

serves 2

calorie count 600kcal; fat content 16g per serving

1 eggplant

1 tablespoon olive oil

juice of ½ lemon

salt and freshly ground black pepper

7 ounces dried rigatoni

8 ounces cherry tomatoes, halved

3 ounces feta cheese, diced

1 tablespoon chopped fresh oregano to garnish

In this recipe, the "sauce" mixture is prepared under the broiler while the pasta is cooking, then mixed together to make a satisfying dish.

Here we have complex carbohydrates for a slow release of energy, plus protein and calcium from the cheese, not to mention potassium, carotene, and vitamins C and E from the tomatoes.

Dice the eggplant into ½-inch cubes, removing and discarding the stem. Combine half of the olive oil with the lemon juice and brush over the eggplant. Alternatively, use an oil-and-water spray (see page 138). Sprinkle the eggplant cubes with salt, then place them in a broiler pan or a roasting pan that will fit under the broiler. Cook under a preheated hot broiler until the cubes are golden brown and tender, moving them around a bit to help them cook evenly. This will take about 10 minutes.

Meanwhile, cook the pasta in a saucepan of rapidly boiling, salted water according to package instructions, until al dente.

When the eggplant is nearly ready, add the tomatoes and feta cheese to the broiler pan, so that you end up with golden brown eggplant, plump, bursting tomatoes, and cheese that is melting and golden brown in places.

Drain the cooked pasta, then return it to the still-warm saucepan, together with the remaining oil. Mix well, then tip the pasta into warmed serving bowls and top with the eggplant, cheese, and tomato mixture, a grinding of black pepper, and some fresh oregano.

Polenta with artichoke hearts and fresh tomato sauce

serves 4

calorie count 320kcal; fat
   content 7g per serving

6 cups water

1½ cups quick-cooking
   polenta

salt and coarsely ground
   black pepper

14-ounce can artichoke
   hearts, drained and
   quartered, or 14 ounces
   frozen artichoke
   bottoms, thawed

4–6 sprigs of flat-leaf
   parsley, roughly
   chopped

½ ounce Parmesan
   cheese, cut into
   thin flakes

for the sauce

1 tablespoon olive oil

1 onion, finely chopped

1 garlic clove, crushed

1 tablespoon sun-dried
   tomato paste

14-ounce can tomatoes
   in juice

salt and freshly ground
   black pepper

In this recipe the polenta is soft, like mashed potatoes, and very comforting and filling it is, too.

Artichokes are a good source of folic acid and potassium and, in addition, they contain cynarin, which is believed to be good for your liver.

Start by making the sauce. Heat the oil in a saucepan, add the onion and garlic, and cook gently for about 7 minutes, until softened but not browned. Add the sun-dried tomato paste, the tomatoes and their juice, breaking them up with a spoon, then cook uncovered for about 15 minutes, until thick.

Meanwhile, boil the water for the polenta in a heavy-bottomed saucepan, preferably non-stick. Tip in the polenta, stirring all the time. Add some salt and pepper and cook for 1 minute, or according to package instructions. Stir in the artichokes and the parsley.

Taste the sauce and season with salt and pepper if necessary. Spoon the polenta on to individual plates, scatter with flakes of Parmesan, and serve with the tomato sauce.

Polenta with mushroom ragout

serves 4

calorie count 320kcal; fat
  content 7g per serving

6 cups water

1½ cups quick-cooking
  polenta or cornmeal

salt and coarsely ground
  black pepper

for the mushroom
  ragout

⅓ ounce dried porcini
  mushrooms

1 tablespoon olive oil

1 onion, finely chopped

2 garlic cloves, crushed

2 pounds mixed fresh
  mushrooms, sliced

¼ cup dry sherry

1 tablespoon soy sauce

salt and freshly ground
  black pepper

chopped fresh parsley
  to garnish

Another dish with soft polenta, this time served with a rich, dark, and tasty mushroom mixture.

The soluble fiber found in polenta keeps hunger pangs at bay, and helps to lower blood cholesterol levels.

Begin making the mushroom ragout. Place the dried porcini mushrooms in a small bowl, cover with boiling water, and let soak. Meanwhile, heat the oil in a saucepan, add the onion and garlic, and cook gently for about 7 minutes, until softened but not browned. Add the fresh mixed mushrooms, sherry, and soy sauce, and stir, then cook, uncovered, over moderate heat. Meanwhile, drain the porcini, reserving the soaking liquid. Chop the porcini—kitchen scissors are good for this—and add to the saucepan of mushrooms. Then strain the porcini soaking liquid into the pan and let the mixture bubble away. The mushrooms will produce their own liquid—lots of it, probably—and you need to cook them until the liquid has mostly boiled away, leaving a thick syrup bathing the tender mushrooms. This will take 15–20 minutes.

When the mushrooms are nearly ready, boil the water for the polenta in a heavy-bottomed saucepan, preferably non-stick. Tip in the polenta, stirring all the time. Add some salt and pepper, and cook for 1 minute, or according to package instructions.

Check the seasoning of the ragout, adding a little salt and pepper if necessary, then spoon the polenta on to individual plates. Top with the mushrooms, sprinkle with a little chopped parsley, and serve.

Bakes and broils

Some of the recipes in this section require a longer cooking time—either in the oven or on top of the stove—than others in this book. However, as the preparation is very quick, and you don't have to do anything to the food during the cooking time, I feel that these recipes are useful time-savers. You cannot turn your back on the broiler in the same way, but the broiled dishes take less time in any case.

Crisp-broiled eggplant slices

serves 2

calorie count 160kcal; fat
    content 3g per serving

1 eggplant

½ cup 0% fat fromage
    frais

½ teaspoon Dijon mustard

½ teaspoon balsamic
    vinegar

salt and freshly ground
    black pepper

1 cup white or brown soft
    fine bread crumbs

2 tablespoons finely
    grated Parmesan
    or Pecorino cheese

oil-and-water spray
    (see page 138)

This is my version of one of Sue Kreitzman's delicious low-fat recipes from her book Low Fat Vegetarian Cookery.

Peel the eggplant and remove the stalk. Cut the eggplant into six ¼-inch thick slices. Place the fromage frais in a bowl and stir in the mustard, balsamic vinegar, and salt and pepper to taste. Sprinkle half the bread crumbs on to a large plate and mix in 1 tablespoon of the grated cheese.

Spread one side of an eggplant slice with the fromage frais mixture then dip in the bread crumb mixture. Coat the other side with fromage frais and bread crumbs in the same way. Place the coated eggplant slice on a broiler pan or in a roasting pan that will fit under your broiler. Repeat with the remaining slices of eggplant.

Spray the eggplant slices with the oil-and-water spray, then place under a preheated broiler and cook for 4–5 minutes, or until crisp and brown. Turn the slices over, spray with the oil and water, and broil until the second side is brown and crisp.

Serve with Low-fat oven "French fries" (see page 105) for a filling meal.

Stuffed ramiro peppers with roast parsnips

serves 2

calorie count 440kcal; fat
   content 18g per serving

2 ramiro peppers

4 ounces cherry tomatoes,
   halved

3 ounces feta cheese,
   cut into ¼-inch dice

4 teaspoons pesto sauce

salt and freshly ground
   black pepper

1 pound small parsnips

2 teaspoons olive oil

juice of ½ lemon

Ramiro peppers are extra sweet red peppers, which look a little like giant red chili peppers. They are thin-fleshed, so they cook quickly, and I find them delectable. Peppers and parsnips might seem a rather strange combination, particularly as they are not really seasonal bed-fellows, but all I can say is do try it, because it works. The sweet starchiness of the parsnips really complements the slight sharpness of the peppers with their tomato-pesto-cheese filling. Also, it is very easy to make. The only other accompaniment needed might be some warm bread or some couscous if you are really hungry.

Loads of nutrients here, including vitamin C, calcium, folic acid, and protein.

Preheat the oven to 400°F. Halve the peppers, cutting through the stems. Remove the seeds, leaving the stems intact. Mix together the cherry tomatoes, feta cheese, and pesto sauce, and season to taste with salt and pepper. Divide this mixture between the four pepper halves and arrange them in a single layer in a shallow baking dish.

Trim the parsnips, then halve or quarter them, depending on their size. Place them in a bowl with the olive oil, lemon juice, and some salt and pepper, and turn them with your hands to coat them evenly with the oil and flavorings. Place the parsnips in a single layer on a baking sheet.

Put the parsnips into the hottest part of your oven. Put the peppers on the oven shelf below the parsnips. Bake for about 35 minutes, until the parsnips are tender and lightly browned, turning them over halfway through the cooking time, and the peppers are tender and full of the delicious juices produced by the pesto, cheese, and tomatoes. Serve at once.

Broiled Mediterranean vegetables with lemon and garlic marinade and couscous

serves 2

calorie count 400kcal; fat content 22g per serving

1 large garlic clove, crushed

2 tablespoons olive oil

juice of ½ lemon

salt and freshly ground black pepper

1 eggplant, cut into batons about 2 x ½ inch

1 large or 2 medium zucchini, cut into batons about 2 x ½ inch

1 large red bell pepper, deseeded and cut into pieces about 2 x ½ inch

1 fennel bulb, outer layer pared as necessary, cut into eighths

1 red or purple onion, cut into eighths

1 cup couscous

You can reduce the calories and fat content in this recipe if you use an oil-and-water spray (see page 138) or one of the low-fat cooking sprays, preferably an olive-oil one, available from supermarkets.

A feast of flavors and vitamins.

Make the marinade by mixing together the crushed garlic, olive oil, lemon juice, and a seasoning of salt and pepper. Brush the marinade all over the prepared vegetables and place them on a broiler pan or a baking sheet that will fit under your broiler.

Place under a preheated broiler and cook for about 20 minutes, or until the vegetables are tender and browned in places, moving them around as necessary. (If your broiler is small, cook them in two or more batches and keep the ones that are done warm in the oven.) Alternatively, you can roast them in the oven as described for the Roasted root vegetables (see page 102).

While the vegetables are cooking, cook the couscous according to the package instructions. Keep it warm in a saucepan over low heat or in a steamer set over a pan of simmering water. Serve the vegetables with the couscous.

Roasted root vegetables

serves 2

calorie count 360kcal; fat
content 5g per serving

1 pound carrots and
   rutabaga, peeled or
   scrubbed, trimmed
1 pound baby potatoes
4 ounces baby onions,
   peeled
2 teaspoons olive oil
juice of ½ lemon
1 large garlic clove,
   crushed
salt and freshly ground
   black pepper

*This is very quick and filling, although you might like to serve it with
a sauce, such as yogurt with some chopped fresh herbs, or hummus
(see page 40); and I often have a few salad leaves on the side, too.*

*A mixture full of vitamins and minerals, including iron, vitamin C,
beta-carotene, and boron for alert brains and healthy bones.*

Preheat the oven to 425°F. Put all the vegetables in a bowl with the
olive oil, lemon juice, garlic, salt and pepper, and turn them with your
hands to coat them evenly with the oil and flavorings.

Spread the vegetables in a single layer on a baking sheet. Place in the
preheated oven and bake for 25–30 minutes, or until golden brown
and tender, turning them over halfway through the cooking time.
Serve immediately.

Cheesy potato bake

serves 2

calorie count 300kcal; fat content 7g per serving

1 pound waxy potatoes, peeled and cut into 1/4-inch slices

2 ounces reduced-fat Cheddar cheese, grated

for the tomato sauce

1 teaspoon olive oil

1 onion, finely chopped

1 garlic clove, crushed

1 tablespoon tomato paste

14-ounce can tomatoes in juice

4 ounces button mushrooms, sliced

salt and freshly ground black pepper

Simple but good and filling. Serve this with a cooked vegetable, such as green beans or quick-to-cook ready-washed spinach, or with a salad of leaves dressed with a drop of olive oil, a squeeze of lemon juice, and some salt and pepper.

Potatoes are a useful source of vitamin C, and the tomatoes provide vitamin E, carotene, and magnesium, which helps the body use calcium (provided by the cheese in this recipe) to create strong bones.

Half fill a saucepan with water for the potatoes and bring to a boil. Cook the potatoes in the boiling water until tender enough for you to insert a knife point into them—they need to be tender but not mushy. Drain well.

Meanwhile, make the tomato sauce. Heat the oil in a saucepan, add the onion and garlic, and cook gently for about 7 minutes, until softened but not browned. Add the tomato paste and the canned tomatoes with their juice, breaking them up with a spoon, and then add the mushrooms. Cook, uncovered, for about 15 minutes, until the liquid has evaporated. Season to taste with salt and pepper.

Arrange half the potato slices in a shallow baking dish that will fit under the broiler. Spoon the tomato sauce over the potatoes and sprinkle with half of the cheese. Then arrange the remaining potatoes in a layer on top, followed by the rest of the cheese. Place under a preheated broiler and cook for 5 minutes, or until the cheese is golden brown and the mixture is heated right through. Serve hot.

Pommes anna

serves 2

calorie count 250kcal; fat content 3.5g per serving

1 pound potatoes, peeled and sliced
1 teaspoon olive oil
1 garlic clove, crushed
freshly grated nutmeg
salt and freshly ground black pepper
½ cup skim milk or soy milk

This is very comforting food, and the preparation is simple—just a bit of peeling and slicing, then put it in the oven and forget about it for an hour. Serve with peas or salad.

Potatoes are a great source of nutrients. One serving of this dish, for instance, provides about half your recommended daily vitamin C and one-third of your vitamin B6, iron, and potassium.

Preheat the oven to 375°F. Put the potato slices in a bowl with the olive oil and garlic, nutmeg, salt and pepper, turning them until the potatoes are coated with the oil.

Arrange the potatoes in layers in a shallow baking dish and pour in the milk to come three-quarters of the way up the potatoes. Cover and bake for 1 hour, or until the potatoes are tender, removing the lid 10–15 minutes before the end of the cooking time to brown the top.

Low-fat oven "French fries"

serves 2

calorie count 225kcal; fat content 2.5g per serving

These make a tasty accompaniment, and I also like them as a main course with a large salad and some mayonnaise, or with white cheese or Golden pepper sauce (see page 38).

1 pound potatoes, peeled and cut into thick batons

1 teaspoon olive oil

sea salt

Preheat the oven to 425°F. Put the potato batons in a bowl with the olive oil and turn them with your hands to coat them evenly with oil.

Spread the potatoes in a single layer on a baking sheet. Place in the oven and bake for 25–30 minutes, or until crisp and golden, turning them halfway through cooking. Sprinkle with salt and serve at once.

wicked desserts
and sweet sauces

Wicked desserts and sweet sauces

The desserts and toppings that follow are fast while being very low in fat, or sugar, or both. They therefore provide a pleasant ending to a meal without ending up on your hips and thighs, or spoiling your intentions to eat healthily!

Although wonderful for a special meal, you don't have to use cream, mascarpone, or crème fraîche to make a dessert that tastes great. Whizzed up in an instant, Ricotta cream (see page 125)—or Bean curd vanilla cream (see page 124) if you don't eat dairy produce—can be used instead of cream. So can Greek yogurt, which is creamy and luscious yet much lower in fat and calories than any of the creams.

There are also some recipes here for simple desserts based on fruit, both fresh and cooked, including some incredibly virtuous yet surprisingly delicious ice creams.

Pears in red wine and ginger

serves 4

calorie count 180kcal; fat content 0g per serving

4 pears
1¼ cups red wine
thinly pared rind and juice of 1 orange
scant ¼ cup sugar
1 tablespoon chopped preserved ginger

Serve these pears with Greek yogurt or Ricotta cream (see page 125).

Peel the pears, keeping them whole and their stems intact. Put the pears into a saucepan with the wine, orange juice, and pared rind. Bring to a boil, then cover and simmer gently until the pears are tender—test them with a skewer—about 30 minutes.

Remove the pears from the pan using a slotted spoon and place them in a shallow dish. Add the sugar and ginger to the wine mixture in the pan and heat gently until the sugar has dissolved. Then boil briskly, uncovered, until the liquid has reduced a little and is slightly syrupy. Pour the syrup over the pears and serve them hot or cold.

Poached tamarillos

serves 2

calorie count 150kcal; fat content 0g per serving

1¼ cups water

4 tamarillos

½ cup sugar

1 vanilla bean

Some people say figs are the sexiest fruit, but the tamarillo gets my vote. Sometimes called "tree tomato", the tamarillo looks like a plastic-skinned Victoria plum. You remove the skin to reveal apricot-colored flesh within, but it is when you pierce this to reveal the jelly-like pulp surrounding the black seeds—a deep, intense vermilion color, bitter-sweet and, I think, like Campari in taste and color—that you grasp the full drama. Serve the poached tamarillos just as they are, or with thick yogurt or Ricotta cream (see page 125).

Bring the water to a boil in a saucepan. Place the tamarillos in the water and simmer gently for 1–2 minutes, or until the skins have loosened. Remove them from the water using a slotted spoon, cool under cold water and peel off the skins, leaving the stems intact.

Add the sugar to the water in the pan and heat gently, without boiling, until the sugar has dissolved. Return the skinned tamarillos to the pan with the vanilla bean. Cook gently for 4–5 minutes, until the tamarillos are tender, then remove the pan from the heat and let the tamarillos steep in the liquid. They can stay there until you are ready to serve them, because they will go on improving. Serve warm or chilled, with a little of the cooking liquid poured over them.

Remove the vanilla bean, wash and dry it for future use.

Rhubarb, strawberry, and star anise compote

serves 4

calorie count 50kcal; fat
content 0.1g per serving

1 pound tender rhubarb,
leaves removed

½ cup sugar

4 star anise

thinly pared rind and juice
of 1 orange

8 ounces strawberries,
hulled and sliced

Late spring rhubarb meets early summer strawberries in this refreshing, subtly spiced compote.

Strawberries are rich in vitamin C and rhubarb is a useful source of potassium and manganese. Don't eat rhubarb too often, though, because it contains oxalic acid, which inhibits the absorption of calcium and iron.

Cut the rhubarb into 1-inch slices, removing any tough threads.

Put the rhubarb in a heavy-bottomed, non-aluminum saucepan with the sugar, star anise, and orange rind and juice. Cover and cook gently until the rhubarb is tender but not mushy—about 5 minutes.

Remove from the heat and add the strawberries, or allow the rhubarb to cool completely before mixing with the strawberries if preferred. Serve warm or cold.

Spiced fruit compote

serves 2

calorie count 200kcal; fat
content 0.1g per serving

1 large Cox or other tart,
crisp apple

1 pear

6 ready-to-eat dried
pitted prunes

6 ready-to-eat dried
apricots

6 ready-to-eat dried figs

grated rind and juice of
1 orange

½ cinnamon stick

walnut-sized piece of fresh
gingerroot, grated

I love ginger and use it often in its various forms in both sweet and savory dishes. Here, fresh gingerroot is used with sweet fruits to make a spicy compote; there is no need to peel it before grating. The sweetness of the dried fruit means you probably won't need any additional sugar. You can simmer the fruits very gently in a heavy-bottomed saucepan, but I think they are better baked in the oven—just put them in and forget about them for an hour, then serve them hot or cooled. I think they are nicest served with a creamy accompaniment, such as Ricotta cream (see page 125), Bean curd vanilla cream (see page 124), Greek yogurt or crème fraîche if you are more relaxed about the fat content.

Dried fruits are little powerhouses of nutrients. A serving of this supplies plentiful iron, calcium, potassium, B vitamins, beta-carotene, and boron—a trace mineral that helps maintain healthy bones.

Preheat the oven to 350°F—or you could choose to simmer the fruit. Cut the apple and pear into chunky pieces, discarding the cores, but leaving the peel on. Place in a casserole dish or heavy-bottomed saucepan with the dried prunes, apricots, figs, orange rind and juice, cinnamon stick, and grated ginger. Cover and cook for 1 hour in the oven, or over low heat—preferably on a heat diffuser if you are cooking the compote on top of the stove—until the fruit is very tender and bathed in its own glossy syrup. Serve warm or cold.

Jelled black cherry compote

serves 4

calorie count 170kcal; fat content 0g per serving

1 pound 6 ounce jar pitted black cherries in light syrup

3 tablespoons sugar

1 tablespoon agar-agar flakes

2 tablespoons brandy

Vegetarian jelled desserts don't always work because the jelling agent adds its own slightly odd flavor and it is difficult to get the right texture. However, this jelled compote is something else altogether—luscious cherries in a soft jelled sauce flavored with brandy. Serve with a dollop of cream or ice cream, depending on your inclination. Incidentally, if you are wondering how a jelled dessert can be quick, make this recipe and you'll see—agar-agar (see page 136) sets rapidly, thickening even as the mixture cools; and this is good to eat when warm and semi-set.

Cherries are rich in potassium, iron, and magnesium.

Tip the cherries and their syrup into a saucepan. Add the sugar and bring to a boil. Sprinkle the agar-agar flakes over the top and stir in; boil for a further 4–5 minutes, then remove from the heat and stir in the brandy. Pour into four bowls or a large serving dish. It will thicken and become softly jelled as it cools. Serve warm, or chill for up to 24 hours.

Satsumas, kiwi fruit, and lychees

serves 2–3

calorie count approx
100–160kcal;
fat content approx
0.5g per serving

I generally use canned rather than fresh lychees, as I love their juicy, translucent perfumed flesh but find them tedious to peel in any quantity. They go well with satsumas and kiwi fruits.

Rich in vitamin C, so just the thing when you feel like a pick-me-up.

14-ounce can lychees
2 satsumas, peeled
2 kiwi fruits, peeled

Drain the lychees, reserving the liquid, and put them in a bowl. (If you wish to remove more of the sugar syrup from the lychees, rinse them in a strainer under the cold faucet.) Cut the satsumas and kiwi fruits into thin slices, catching any juice, and add them to the bowl. Moisten the fruit mixture with a little of the lychee liquid if you think it needs it, and serve at once or chill for up to 4 hours.

Strawberry ice

serves 6

calorie count 100kcal; fat
content 0.1g per serving

Smooth, icy, and refreshing. The frozen strawberries freeze the buttermilk and the food processor churns it all to a cream.

Strawberries contain higher levels of vitamin C than any other berry; eating them after iron-rich foods, such as lentils, will enable your body to make the fullest use of the iron.

1 pound frozen
strawberries
4–6 heaped tablespoons
sugar
1¼ cups buttermilk
sprigs of fresh mint

Put the strawberries in a blender or food processor with 4–5 heaped tablespoons sugar and the buttermilk. Whiz to a thick cream. Taste and add a little more sugar if needed.

Serve at once, decorated with sprigs of fresh mint.

Banana ice

serves 1

calorie count 90kcal; fat
content 0.5g per serving

1 large banana,
not too ripe

1 teaspoon pure
vanilla extract

Frozen and puréed bananas make the most unctuous, luxurious cream. I keep some chunks of banana ready-frozen in the freezer and whiz this up in an instant if I get a craving for ice cream, or I might make the more luxurious chocolate version (opposite)—both incredibly low in fat and positively good for you. In fact, the more you eat low-fat foods, the less you fancy the high-fat options and, believe me, I never thought I would say that.

You can jazz up the "ice cream" by scattering the top with some very finely grated high-cocoa-solids chocolate or a spoonful of Chocolate sauce (see page 124) or Raspberry sauce (see page 125), or a crushed amaretti biscuit, but it is very good just as it is.

Research shows that people who regularly eat potassium-rich food, such as bananas, can lower their risk of having a stroke by as much as 40 per cent.

Peel the banana and cut it into even slices, about ½ inch thick. Spread them out on a plate or baking sheet and place in the freezer, uncovered, until solid—about 1 hour.

When solid, place the chunks in a blender or food processor with the vanilla and whiz, scraping down the sides a couple of times, until you have a thick, smooth cream. Scoop into a bowl and eat at once.

If you don't want to make the ice cream immediately, loosen the frozen banana chunks from their plate or baking sheet, put into a freezer bag or other airtight container, and store in the freezer for up to 2 weeks.

Banana chocolate maple ice

serves 1

calorie count 200kcal; fat content 5g per serving

1 banana, not too ripe

1 tablespoon 0% fat Greek yogurt

2 tablespoons pure maple syrup

1 teaspoon unsweetened low-fat cocoa powder

½ teaspoon pure vanilla extract

½ ounce high-cocoa-solids semisweet chocolate, very finely grated

1 teaspoon chopped toasted hazelnuts

Once you start using frozen banana chunks you'll probably think of all kinds of variations on the theme. This is one of my favorites. Instead of the hazelnuts, you could top this with 2 crushed amaretti. For a vegan version, soy milk works well instead of the yogurt.

Real comfort food with the minimum of fat and one-quarter of the day's potassium requirement.

Peel the banana, cut into chunks and freeze until solid, as described for Banana ice (see opposite).

Just before you want to eat the ice cream, put the banana chunks in a blender or food processor with the yogurt, maple syrup, cocoa powder, and vanilla extract, and whiz to a thick cream, stopping the machine once or twice and scraping down the sides as necessary.

Scoop into a bowl, sprinkle with the grated chocolate and chopped hazelnuts, and serve at once.

Apricot bean curd fool

serves 4

calorie count 120kcal; fat content 4g per serving

8–10-ounce package of plain bean curd

¾ cup ready-to-eat dried apricots or soaked and cooked dried apricots

1 tablespoon clear honey

slivered almonds or 2 crushed amaretti, to decorate

If you want to eat more bean curd, perhaps for health reasons (see page 8), whizzing it into a creamy fool with a flavorsome fruit, such as dried apricots or mango, is one easy way. I have reservations about the additives used to produce no-need-to-soak dried fruit, but I must admit these ready-to-eat dried fruits are useful when you are in a hurry. When there is time though, I recommend using organic dried apricots without preservatives. Soak them in water for an hour or more—overnight is good—then simmer them gently, perhaps with a vanilla bean, for 45–60 minutes until really tender.

A very nutritious dessert, being rich in iron, calcium, beta-carotene, and vitamin E; creamy but very low in saturated fats, and cholesterol-free.

Cut the bean curd into chunks and put into a blender or food processor with the apricots and honey. Whiz thoroughly until all the apricots are puréed and you have a thick cream. Spoon into small bowls or glasses. Serve at once or chill for up to 24 hours. Decorate with slivered almonds or crushed amaretti just before serving.

Raspberry brûlée

serves 4

calorie count 150kcal; fat content 3g per serving

1 pound fresh or frozen raspberries, thawed

sugar to taste

1 quantity of Ricotta cream (see page 125)

4 tablespoons granulated brown sugar

Delectable with raspberries, this also works well with strawberries, blueberries, frozen mixed berry fruits, skinned ripe peaches or nectarines and, surprisingly perhaps, bananas.

Raspberries are rich in vitamin C for healthy skin, bones, and teeth; this vitamin also speeds up the body's healing processes and ability to absorb iron.

Place the raspberries in a shallow heatproof dish and sweeten to taste with a little sugar. Spread the Ricotta cream over the top to cover the raspberries, then sprinkle with the granulated brown sugar.

Place the dish under a preheated hot broiler for 30–60 seconds, to caramelize the sugar. Let cool for a moment or two before serving.

Lemon cheesecake with chocolate ginger crumb case

serves 4–6

calorie count
140–200kcal;
fat content 3–4g
per serving

for the crumb case

1 ounce high-cocoa-solids
semisweet chocolate,
broken into pieces

2 ounces amaretti

2 ounces crunchy wheat
and malted barley
breakfast cereal,
such as Grape Nuts

2 teaspoons ground ginger

for the filling

1 pound quark or low-fat
soft cheese

2 tablespoons sugar

finely grated rind of
2 lemons

4 tablespoons lemon curd

This is a very quick cheesecake, which is low in fat and calories but silky-textured and full of flavor. Do use a good-quality, homemade-style lemon curd, organic if possible.

First make the crumb case. Melt the chocolate in a small bowl set over a saucepan of gently simmering water, or in the microwave. Put the amaretti and cereal in a blender or food processor and reduce to fine crumbs. Add the ground ginger and melted chocolate; whiz until the crumbs are coated with chocolate and hold together. Spread this mixture inside a 7-inch diameter tart ring placed on a flat plate from which you can serve the cheesecake.

For the filling, whisk together the quark, sugar, and lemon rind until smooth and light. Add the lemon curd and mix it in gently but not thoroughly, streaking the cheese mixture with lemon ripples. Spread the cheesecake mixture over the chocolate crumb case. Serve immediately, or chill for an hour or so.

To serve, simply lift off the tart ring, leaving a neat cheesecake that looks as if it took much longer to make than it did and tastes far richer than it is!

Variation: Blackcurrant cheesecake
Swirl the quark and lemon rind mixture with 4 tablespoons blackcurrant preserve instead of lemon curd.

Ricotta cream with candied fruits and chocolate sauce

serves 2

calorie count 410kcal; fat content 16g per serving

4 ounces ricotta cheese

4 ounces quark cheese

1 teaspoon pure vanilla extract

1 tablespoon sugar

½ cup chopped mixed candied fruits of different colors

4 tablespoons Chocolate sauce (see page 124)

Fresh, rich-tasting ricotta cream, bejewelled with candied fruits, in a pool of rich chocolate sauce.

Whisk the ricotta, quark, vanilla extract, and sugar together in a bowl or whiz in a blender or food processor until smooth and light. Fold the chopped candied fruits into the ricotta cream, leaving a few pieces for decoration.

Divide the chocolate sauce between two plates; spoon the ricotta cream on top, and decorate with the remaining candied fruits.

Variation: Ginger ricotta in chocolate sauce

Omit the sugar, vanilla, and candied fruits. Whisk or blend the cheeses with 2 tablespoons of ginger preserve, then fold in 2 ounces chopped preserved ginger, drained of its syrup.

Chocolate sauce

makes about ⅔ cup

calorie count 25kcal;
   fat content 1.5g
    per tablespoon

1 ounce high-cocoa-solids
   semisweet chocolate
⅔ cup water
2 tablespoons sugar
2 tablespoons low-fat
   cocoa powder
1 tablespoon pure vanilla
   extract

This sauce is intensely flavored, quick to make, and low in fat. High-cocoa-solids chocolate is widely available and most supermarkets stock it. Read the label and look for 70 or 75% cocoa solids—the higher the cocoa solids, the lower the fat content.

Chocolate is believed to boost serotonin and endorphin levels in the brain, giving that feel-good effect. It is also a useful source of iron and magnesium.

Cut or break the chocolate into small pieces and place them in a heavy-bottomed saucepan with the water, sugar, cocoa powder, and vanilla extract. Stir to blend the cocoa, then heat gently until the sugar and chocolate have dissolved. Increase the heat and simmer briskly for 1 minute, then remove from the heat. Serve hot or cold.

Tofu vanilla cream

serves 4

calorie count 150kcal; fat
   content 3.5g per serving

8–10-ounce package of
   plain bean curd
1 tablespoon clear honey
   or pure maple syrup
1 tablespoon pure vanilla
   extract
1–2 tablespoons water

If you want a light, creamy, dairy-free topping, then this is the one for you. Sweeten according to your taste, but don't stint on the vanilla extract.

Numerous large-scale studies have shown that eating bean curd can reduce the risk of cancer—see also page 8.

Cut the bean curd into rough chunks and place in a blender or food processor with the honey or maple syrup, and the vanilla extract. Whiz to a thick purée, adding a little water to make it thinner if you wish. Serve immediately, or chill until required.

Raspberry sauce

serves 4

calorie count 40–50kcal;
   fat content
   0g per serving

1 pound fresh or frozen
   raspberries, thawed
2–3 tablespoons sugar
1–2 tablespoons water

It is a pity that raspberry sauce, or coulis, has become such a culinary cliché in smart foodie circles, because it is very good and also useful. It is gorgeous poured around pale-colored fruits, such as pieces of sweet green-fleshed melon, for instance, or over ice cream or sorbet. Anyway, unfashionable or not, I make it, love it, eat it, freeze it…here is the simple recipe.

Delicate and delectable, raspberries are rich in vitamin C—just one cupful gives you around half your recommended daily dose.

Purée the raspberries in a blender or food processor, then push them through a strainer to remove the seeds. Sweeten the resulting sauce with sugar to taste and add a little water to make it thinner if you wish.

Ricotta cream

makes 8 ounces

calorie count 300kcal;
   fat content 11.5g for
   the whole quantity

4 ounces ricotta cheese
4 ounces quark cheese
1 tablespoon sugar
½ teaspoon pure vanilla
   extract

In her book **Low Fat Desserts,** *Sue Kreitzman recommends mixing ricotta and quark cheese for a well-balanced flavor, and I agree. The two low-fat cheeses work really well together. The resulting vanilla-flavored topping has less than 4% fat; compare this with Greek yogurt at 9%, light cream at around 20%, and heavy cream at 46%.*

Both cheeses provide plenty of calcium for healthy teeth and bones.

Place all the ingredients in a bowl and whisk together by hand or whiz in a blender or food processor until smooth and light.

G K B

X$_8$ Q$_{10}$ N$_1$ R

cool cakes

Cool cakes

The recipes in this section are, like all the others in the book, fast to make and relatively healthy, being particularly good sources of vitamins and minerals.

You don't need any fancy equipment to make these cakes, although I do recommend using non-stick or silicon baking paper for lining cake pans, which means that you don't have to grease the pans and the cakes come out of, or off, them like magic. There is also a gray non-stick fabric available for lining cake pans, which you can use and re-use. Just lay it on your baking sheet or cut it to fit the pans, as you would paper, and you can re-use it many times.

Golden raisin tea bread

makes 10 slices
calorie count 160kcal; fat
content 1.2g per slice

8 ounces golden raisins
1¼ cups strong tea
½ cup light brown sugar,
   plus extra 1–2
   teaspoons for sprinkling
1¼ cups self-rising whole
   wheat flour
⅓ cup brown rice flour
1 egg, beaten

This is sweet, moist, low in fat, and very quick and easy to make—as long as you remember to soak the dried fruit overnight. If you can't get brown rice flour, use extra self-rising whole wheat flour instead.

Rich in magnesium, calcium, iron, and potassium: a great pick-me-up.

Put the golden raisins in a bowl, cover with the tea and leave overnight. The next day, preheat the oven to 325°F. Line a 6 x 4 inch loaf pan with a strip of non-stick paper.

Add all the remaining ingredients to the bowl of tea-soaked raisins and mix well. Spoon into the prepared loaf pan and sprinkle the top with the extra sugar. Bake for 1¼ hours, until a skewer inserted into the middle comes out clean.

Let cool in the pan for 10 minutes, then invert on to a wire rack to finish cooling. Cut into 10 fairly thick slices and serve as it is, or buttered.

Cornmeal and olive muffins

makes 10

calorie count 150kcal; fat
content 6g per muffin

1¼ cups cornmeal flour

1¼ cups all-purpose flour

2 teaspoons baking
powder

½ teaspoon baking soda

2 eggs

1 tablespoon sugar

2 tablespoons corn,
soy or canola oil

⅔ cup skim milk
or soy milk

3 ounces pitted black
or green olives

Muffins are quick to make—simply divide your ingredients into dry and liquid, mix them together quickly and lumpily, spoon into paper cases, and bake.

These muffins contain soluble fiber from the cornmeal—thought to help lower blood cholesterol—and iron from the olives.

Preheat the oven to 400°F. Place paper muffin cases in 10 muffin-pan cups—or grease the cups.

Put the cornmeal in a bowl and sift in the flour with the baking powder and baking soda. In another bowl, whisk together the eggs, sugar, oil, and milk, then pour into the bowl of dry ingredients and stir together roughly, using a fork, until the powdery flour has just disappeared—don't over-work the mixture. Quickly stir in the olives, then spoon the mixture into the paper cases or muffin-pan cups to three-quarters fill them.

Bake for about 20 minutes, or until risen and firm. If you have baked them directly in the muffin pan, without paper cases, let the muffins cool before removing them from the pan.

Blueberry muffins

makes 10

calorie count 170kcal; fat
    content 4.5g per muffin

1½ cups all-purpose flour

2 teaspoons baking
    powder

½ teaspoon baking soda

2 eggs

scant ½ cup sugar

2 tablespoons corn,
    soy or canola oil

grated rind of 1 lemon

⅔ cup skim milk
    or soy milk

3½ ounces fresh
    blueberries

This is a very adaptable mixture to which you can add your favorite flavorings. Paper muffin cases make life simpler. The muffins are best eaten the same day, although they do freeze well.

Being fairly low in fat, muffins make a healthy snack food.

Preheat the oven to 400°F. Place paper muffin cases in 10 muffin-pan cups—or grease the cups.

Sift the flour into a bowl with the baking powder and baking soda. In another bowl, whisk together the eggs, sugar, oil, lemon rind, and milk, then pour into the bowl of dry ingredients and stir together roughly, using a fork, until all the powdery flour has just disappeared—don't over-work the mixture. Quickly stir in the blueberries, then spoon the mixture into the paper cases or directly into the muffin-pan cups to three-quarters fill them.

Bake for about 20 minutes, or until risen and firm. If you have baked them directly in the muffin pan, without paper cases, let the muffins cool before removing from the pan.

Variation: Apricot and wheatgerm muffins
Replace ¼ cup of the flour with ¼ cup wheatgerm; use the rind of an orange instead of a lemon and ⅔ cup chopped ready-to-eat dried apricots instead of blueberries.

Variation: Skinny double chocolate muffins
Replace ¼ cup of the flour with ¼ cup unsweetened low-fat cocoa powder. Omit the lemon rind and add 1–2 teaspoons of vanilla extract to the liquid ingredients. Instead of blueberries, add 2 ounces chopped high-cocoa-solids chocolate or chocolate chips.

Fruity rock cakes

makes 12

calorie count 200kcal; fat content 10g per cake

1½ cups self-rising flour—white, whole wheat, or a mixture
2 teaspoons baking powder
1 teaspoon apple pie spice
3 tablespoons light brown sugar, plus extra for sprinkling
1 cup seedless raisins or mixed dried fruit
grated rind of 1 lemon (optional)
8 tablespoons canola or soy oil
1 egg, beaten
2 tablespoons water

My mother always used to make these but I had forgotten how delicious they were—and how quick to make—until I started experimenting with recipes for this book. You can make them from storecupboard ingredients and, as well as being crunchy, light, and delicious to eat, they are actually good for you, especially if you use whole wheat flour. Flavor them with lemon rind and/or apple pie spice, depending on what is available. You can also vary the fruit content—I love them with plenty of candied peel and some chopped candied ginger. They are also nice made with fresh blueberries instead of raisins and served warm from the oven as a dessert.

These cakes are a useful source of iron from the dried fruit, as well as B vitamins.

Preheat the oven to 400°F. Grease one or two large baking sheets or line with non-stick paper or a liner (see page 128).

Sift the flour, baking powder, and spice into a bowl and add the sugar, dried fruit, and lemon rind, if using. In another bowl, whisk together the oil, egg, and water, then pour this into the dry ingredients and mix together quickly to a crumbly mixture that just holds together.

Place 12 dollops of the mixture on your prepared baking sheet or sheets, allowing a little space around each as they will spread slightly as they cook. Sprinkle a little extra sugar over the top of each, then bake for 15 minutes, until golden brown and crisp.

Let cool on a wire rack. They are lovely warm, and best eaten within a day or so.

Sticky ginger cake

makes 12 pieces

calorie count 190kcal; fat
content 1.2g per piece

5 tablespoons prune
purée (see right)

1 cup light brown sugar

grated rind of 1 lemon

2 eggs

1 cup all-purpose whole
wheat flour

2 teaspoons ground ginger

½ teaspoon baking
powder

⅔ cup golden raisins

2 tablespoons chopped
preserved ginger

3 tablespoons boiling
water

In this quick-to-make, sweet, and gooey cake, the fat is replaced by prune purée, which has the curious ability to behave like fat in cake mixtures. You can make your own purée by steaming some pitted prunes for 10–15 minutes, until they are very soft and tender, then mashing them to break them up and create a purée. Alternatively, you can buy jars of ready-made purée.

Prunes are rich in iron, vitamin B6, and also boron, the trace element that plays a crucial role in calcium absorption and helps us synthesize vitamin D, calcium, and magnesium, for healthy bones.

Preheat the oven to 325°F. Line the base of an 8-inch square cake pan with non-stick paper.

In a large bowl, mix the prune purée with the sugar and lemon rind. Then add the eggs and whisk until everything is well blended. Sift the flour, ground ginger, and baking powder into the prune mixture, finally tipping in the bran left in the strainer or sifter. Mix well, then gently stir in the golden raisins, stem ginger, and boiling water.

Pour the mixture into the prepared cake pan and bake for 40–45 minutes, until the top springs back when lightly touched and a skewer inserted into the center comes out clean.

Let the cake cool in the pan, then cut into squares and remove from the pan.

Sunflower and molasses flapjacks

makes 12

calorie count 150kcal; fat content 7g per flapjack

⅓ cup molasses

scant ⅓ cup all-purpose whole wheat flour

1¼ cups quick-cooking oats

4 tablespoons light brown sugar

3 tablespoons sunflower seeds

3 tablespoons pumpkin seeds

4 tablespoons soy or canola oil

You might not want to over-indulge on these, at 150 calories a throw, but when you do fancy something sweet, these flapjacks will give you a big nutrient boost as the calories are far from being empty ones.

Molasses is a treasure trove of nutrients, including iron and calcium.

Preheat the oven to 400°F. Line an 8-inch square cake pan with non-stick paper.

Warm the can of molasses slightly by placing it in the oven for a few minutes or by standing the can in a saucepan of boiling water. This will make it more liquid and therefore easier to pour out to measure. Use a large measuring pitcher and then you can just add the flour, oats, sugar, sunflower seeds, and pumpkin seeds straight into it. Add the oil, then stir everything together.

Spoon this mixture into the prepared cake pan and press down. Bake for 8–10 minutes, or until slightly risen and crisp. Let cool in the pan, then cut into 12 pieces. The flapjacks will keep for at least a week if stored in an airtight container.

Skinny chocolate brownies

makes 12

calorie count 85kcal; fat content 1g per brownie

All the flavor of traditional brownies with none of the fat, and with the feel-good properties of chocolate. Serve them cold as a dessert, perhaps with a dollop of thick yogurt, or as cakes with tea or coffee.

¼ cup chopped hazelnuts

8 egg whites

½ cup sugar

1½ teaspoons pure vanilla extract

⅓ cup all-purpose flour

1 tablespoon cocoa powder

confectioners' sugar for dredging

Preheat the oven to 350°F. Line the base of an 8-inch square pan with non-stick paper. Sprinkle the chopped hazelnuts over the bottom of the pan.

In a large bowl, whisk the egg whites until they stand in stiff peaks, then add the sugar and vanilla extract and whisk again until glossy. Sift the flour and cocoa powder over the egg whites and then fold in gently using a metal spoon. Pour the mixture into the prepared pan and bake for 35–40 minutes, until set.

Let cool in the pan, then cut into squares and remove from the pan. Dredge in confectioners' sugar.

Shopping notes

Agar-agar

Also called kanten, this is a vegetable gel that has been used for over a thousand years. I prefer the flaked form, which you can buy from some health-food stores—especially those with a good macrobiotic section.

Alfalfa

Alfalfa sprouts can be found in the salad section of some supermarkets, or you can buy the seeds from a health-food store and sprout your own. Put 2 tablespoons of the seeds into a large jar, add water to cover the seeds, then cover the opening of the jar with a piece of cheesecloth or other fine cloth and secure it with an elastic band. Let soak over night. The next day, drain off the water and put the jar in a dark place. Rinse and drain the seeds twice a day. After 3–4 days, bring into the light for one final day; rinse and eat.

Amaretti

These crisp, almond-flavored Italian cookies are not only delicious but also surprisingly low in fat (7–8%). They are available from large supermarkets as well as Italian specialty grocery stores—look for the type made from apricot kernels.

Bean curd

I love bean curd. I love the fact that it is a traditional protein food that the Chinese have been making for thousands of years; the way it absorbs flavors, both sweet and savory; the delicacy of its texture and the way it becomes crisp when fried; and its creaminess when puréed. I love the fact that it is such a good source of protein and other nutrients while being pretty low in fat. And I love it because, as with other soy products, such as soy milk, it contains high amounts of phytoestrogens (see page 8). Check with the manufacturers to see if they are using GMO-free soy beans.

Buttermilk

A creamy, cultured milk product, very low in fat and calories.

Chocolate

The higher the cocoa solids content, the lower the percentage of fat. Look for at least 60% cocoa solids.

Coconut milk

Coconut milk is extracted from the flesh of fresh coconuts. It is sold in cans, or in powder form to which you just add water, and is available from supermarkets, delis, and ethnic food stores. Creamed coconut is sold in little blocks that keep for months in the fridge. You can dissolve small pieces of creamed coconut in hot soups and sauces for a rich coconut flavor.

Couscous

Couscous, a wheat product, is sold in health and specialty food stores and supermarkets. It is one of the quickest cooking of the starchy accompaniments.

Curry paste

Asian Indian specialty food stores should carry this. There are so many different types available that it is really a case of trying them to find your own favorite. Read the label to make sure that it is a vegetarian or vegan version.

Fats and oils	For flavor and—just as importantly—because I like to use natural foods, the only fats I use for general cooking are extra virgin olive oil, preferably organic when I can get it; toasted sesame oil (to flavor Asian stir-fries), and unsalted butter. There are no deep-fried recipes in this book and I rarely deep-fry, but when I do I use canola, soy or peanut oil (always making sure they are free of genetically modified organisms or GMOs—see page 8) because these oils are chemically more stable at high temperatures and thus less likely to produce free radicals, which are damaging to health.
Fromage frais	This light, soft, fresh white cheese is the consistency of very thick yogurt and is used in desserts, dressings, and sauces. It is produced with various percentages of fat, including virtually fat-free, which is useful if you are trying to keep fat levels low in your cooking.
Ginger	Smooth juicy knobs of fresh gingerroot are widely available. I have rather lazily discovered that you don't need to peel fresh gingerroot before grating it, but if I am cutting it into thin shreds or tiny pieces I do peel it first. Preserved ginger in syrup is useful for flavoring cakes and desserts, as is candied ginger. I also like to include some pickled ginger in Japanese-style recipes. You can buy this—it looks like pretty pink ribbons—in some health food stores, macrobiotic stockists, and Japanese food stores.
Grape Nuts	This is a breakfast cereal consisting of little crunchy nuggets, the size of coarse bread crumbs, made from malted wheat and barley. I think it is an acquired taste for breakfast, but powdered in a food processor it makes good, low-fat, crunchy crumbs for crumb case flans—a tip for which I have Sue Kreitzman and her book **Low Fat Desserts** to thank.
Hoisin sauce	This Chinese sauce is made from fermented soy beans, spices, and garlic, and is available from Chinese food stores and supermarkets. You need to check the source of the soy beans it contains if you wish to avoid GMOs—see page 8.
Madeira	Like sherry (see below), this fortified wine is very useful for adding that extra something to dishes; I love adding it to tasty gravies and stews (see page 67).
Matzo meal	Matzos are unleavened (yeast-free) crackers that replace leavened bread during the Jewish Passover. When ground to meal, they make a useful thickening agent.
Mirin	A sweet, fortified Japanese rice wine, available from Chinese and Japanese food stores and some large supermarkets. For trying out the occasional Japanese recipe, I think medium sherry is a satisfactory substitute.

Miso	This is a Japanese fermented soy bean paste, which will keep for months in the fridge. The best miso is organic and unpasteurized. There are several types, of varying strengths and shades, from cream-colored to dark brown—my own preference is for the lighter, sweeter type. You might find miso among the specialty foods in a large supermarket or in a health-food store with a good macrobiotic section.
Molasses	Molasses is dark and thick as tar, and a rich source of nutrients—in particular calcium and iron. It keeps for ages in a cool dry place.
Noodles	The quickest to cook—they need only soaking in hot water before use—are the very thin white Chinese rice noodles, sometimes called vermicelli or stir-fry noodles. They are available from some large supermarkets and Chinese food stores. Vacuum-packed fresh egg noodles, in medium or fine widths, take only 3–4 minutes to cook. They are available from most large supermarkets and ethnic food stores.
Nori	This laver seaweed usually comes in the form of thin sheets, often used to wrap sweetened, vinegared rice, or sushi. Nori is a highly nutritious ingredient, which keeps well in the cupboard. You can buy it untoasted or ready-toasted from health-food stores with a good macrobiotic section, or from Chinese and Japanese food stores. It is probably only a matter of time before it is available from the special ingredients departments of supermarkets. To bring out its flavor, nori should be toasted before use: using tongs, hold it over a gas flame for a few seconds; ready-toasted nori is useful if you have an electric stove. Once toasted, nori can be crumbled over Japanese-style dishes or used as a base for rice and vegetables.
Oil spray	For greasing pans and skillets with the minimum amount of fat and calories, an oil spray (available from supermarkets) can be useful if you are trying to keep your fat intake very low indeed. Another way of reducing the quantity of fat you use is to follow Sue Kreitzman's tip of putting some olive oil into a spray bottle (I use a small one designed for spraying house plants) and topping it up with water—perhaps one part oil to eight or ten parts water, or less, depending on how much you want to reduce your fat usage. Shake well, then spray.
Passata	Passata (Italian strained tomatoes) is available from some supermarkets and Italian food stores.
Polenta	Quick-cooking, often called "instant", polenta (finely ground cornmeal) is now widely available; many supermarkets stock it.
Porcini mushrooms, dried	Leathery strips of dried, sliced porcini mushrooms (ceps) are quite easy to find in supermarkets and Italian food stores. They are often sold in small packages holding

about ⅓ ounce, which is just about right for adding to a dish for two people. They add smoky depth to food and I particularly like them in risotto, along with mushroom stock (see page 88).

Quark	This virtually fat-free soft cheese is thicker than fromage frais—it is more like cream cheese without the fat content or rich, creamy flavor; its own flavor is milky and slightly sharp.
Rice	Basmati rice, with its short, pointy grains, cooks the fastest, so is the type I tend to use when I'm short of time. Even brown basmati takes only 20 minutes or so to cook. It is always useful to have a package of round-grain rice—arborio or carnaroli—to make a quick risotto.
Rice drink	A lactose-free "milky" drink, available plain or flavored from health-food stores and in some supermarkets.
Ricotta	This Italian curd cheese contains around 10% fat. It has a fuller flavor than quark (see above) but works well mixed with it half and half to produce a creamy cheese with just 5% fat.
Saffron	Buy saffron in the form of stamens rather than powder, so that you know what you are getting. (If you find yourself in Istanbul, bring some back from the market because it is a bargain—even without haggling.).
Sake	This Japanese rice wine, for which medium sherry can be substituted, is sold in Asian food stores and some large supermarkets. It is used in stir-fries and other recipes.
Salt	You cannot beat sea salt for flavor and my favorite is crunchy Maldon, which comes in flaky crystals that you can crumble with your fingers. However, for health reasons, most of us need to reduce our sodium intake and recently I have been experimenting with low-sodium salts. Solo Low Sodium Sea Salt has a good flavor.
Seaweed, powdered	You can buy this from Japanese food stores, for sprinkling over the top of food just before serving. Rich in nutrients, it has the pleasantly salty tang of the sea.
Sesame seeds	Health-food stores will sell the dull, brown–gray sesame seeds, which have been mechanically hulled; I use these rather than the shiny, ivory-colored type, which have often been chemically treated to remove their husks.
Sherry	Dry or medium sherry is useful for perking up dishes, especially if they contain mushrooms. I tend to buy a supermarket's own brand to keep handy for cooking.

Shiitake mushrooms	You can buy dried shiitake mushrooms from the usual sources of Japanese/Chinese products. Soaked in water, then snipped into shreds, they add flavor and texture to casseroles, stir-fries, and rice dishes. Fresh shiitake mushrooms, which you can sometimes buy from supermarkets, have a chewy yet delicate, jell-like texture which I particularly like.
Soy flour	This is useful for adding to dishes, particularly cakes, in place of some of the other flour if you want to boost your phytoestrogen level (see page 8). It is available from health-food stores—do look for an organic brand.
Soy milk	I always use this in place of cow's milk as I have come to love its clean flavor. It is naturally low in fat, although in cooking it produces a surprisingly creamy result. For general cooking, choose unsweetened soy milk. Buy milk made from that is guaranteed free of genetically modified organisms (GMOs); I use Provamel soy milk. Provamel also makes what I consider to be an excellent soy cream; it is similar to light cream and you can achieve a sour cream effect by stirring in 1–2 teaspoons of lemon juice or vinegar until it thickens.
Soy sauce	This seems to bring out the flavor of savory foods. Kikkoman is a reliable brand; I also very much like the Japanese shoyu and tamari (which is wheat-free); both taste less salty than most Chinese soy sauces.
Stock	If you are boiling tasty vegetables, such as leeks, carrots, or celery, save the water for stock. I used to keep a pitcher in my fridge which I filled with vegetable water in this way. These days I tend to steam, broil, bake, or braise vegetables much more and to rely on my instant "cheating" stock (see page 28) or Marigold vegetable bouillon, which is now available from some supermarkets as well as health-food stores. I have recently used some organic stock cubes made by Kallo and particularly liked the mushroom ones, which are great for risotto.
Sun-dried tomato paste	This has a more rounded flavor than ordinary tomato paste but is also considerably higher in calories and fat. It is available from some supermarkets and specialty delis.
Tahini	A cream of puréed sesame seeds, with a wonderfully thick, palate-coating texture and addictive bitterness, that is packed with nutrients. It is high in calories, however, so unless you are trying to boost these—and tahini is excellent for that, very nurturing for the nursing mother, for instance—use it sparingly. Buy the pale, golden-beige tahini: the darker type is too bitter.
Tamari	See Soy sauce.

Teriyaki sauce This is similar to a spicy soy sauce; it is made from soy sauce brewed with wine and spices. Kikkoman makes a good one called Teriyaki Marinade.

Thai curry paste You have to look hard for a vegetarian/vegan Thai curry paste (without any fish products). Cook some vegetables in a can of coconut milk and a teaspoonful of this, serve with Thai scented rice (or ordinary rice), and you have a meal in moments.

Vanilla Fat, juicy vanilla beans are a joy to use. Keep one—or several—plunged into a jar of sugar to scent the sugar with vanilla and keep the bean handy for infusing in milk or sugar syrups with fruit. After use, rinse the vanilla bean, leave it for a few hours to dry, then put it back into the sugar ready for the next time.

Yeast flakes Flakes of inactive (i.e. not baking!) yeast, manufactured by Marigold of Switzerland, are available from health-food stores. They have a cheesy flavor and are an excellent way to add nutrients (especially B vitamins) to foods. They can be added to dishes or sprinkled over the top.

Yogurt For cooking I use plain organic yogurt: cow's milk/ewe's milk/soy milk yogurt are interchangeable here.

It is easy to make your own yogurt. Measure your milk into a wide-necked vacuum flask, then tip the milk into a saucepan and bring to a boil; remove from the heat and let cool to blood temperature. Meanwhile, fill the flask with boiling water to sterilize and warm it. When the milk has cooled sufficiently, drain the water out of the vacuum flask. Whisk a little live cow's milk or soy milk yogurt—store-bought or from a previous batch—into the milk in the saucepan: about 2 rounded teaspoons for every 2 cups. Pour this into the flask, cover, and leave undisturbed for 6–8 hours. For a time the yogurt will get thicker and better the more batches you make, but eventually the "starter" won't work so well and you will need to begin again with a little fresh yogurt.

Index

Acknowledgements

I would like to express my warm thanks to everyone who has been involved in the creation of this book. The idea was cooked up over lunch with Michael Dover and Susan Haynes of Cassell. Susan then put together the brilliant team who made the recipes look so wonderful: photographer Scott Sandford, food stylist Sue Hutchings and art director Lucy Holmes. Lucy has also made a beautiful job of designing the book. The editors, Jo Lethaby and Maggie Ramsay, worked hard on the editing, and Maggie and I spent more than a few hours poring over our respective copies of McCance and Widdowson's *The Composition of Foods*, the nutritionist's "bible", checking the calorie and fat counts, and I also got much useful information from *The Encyclopedia of Vegetarian Living* by Peter Cox (Bloomsbury, 1994). Finally, as ever, I'd like to thank my family, friends, and my agent, Barbara Levy, for their enthusiasm and support.